The I

Maralinga

Operation Buffalo
1956

"You Will Be Safe"

Reg Simpson

The Long Road To Maralinga

Operation Buffalo
1956

"You Will Be Safe"

Reg Simpson

Published by Reg Simpson
2014

First Printing: 2014

ISBN 978-1-291-92734-4

For all information contact:

Reg Simpson via email: regsimp@gmx.com

Dedication

In memory of all those participants of the British Nuclear tests programmes over the years, who suffered with their radiation linked illnesses and unfortunately did not make it this far.

We should not forget also:

Those veterans who today are still suffering with their radiation linked illnesses, 58 years on.

In addition, the descendant children and grandchildren of veterans, who are suffering with genetic illnesses that are, linked to the aforementioned British Nuclear programmes.

The British Government may have cast you aside, but your colleagues remember you with respect.

There, but for the grace of God, go I.

Contents

Acknowledgements

I thank the British government and the Royal Air Force for their input. They made it possible for me to have the unique experience of being a part of Operation Buffalo in 1956, with all the hazards that went with it. I thank them also for the honour of knowing that, I am one of the surviving British Nuclear Test Veterans from that era.

Lastly, my thanks go to a very important member of the team, my wife Brenda. I greatly appreciate her tolerance, fortitude and support, especially when I frequently disappear into another room in the house, to continue the writing of my memoirs, of which, this is but a small portion.

Preface

This is a true account of a short period in my life, for which I both curse and thank the political establishment in this great country of ours, namely the successive British governments from 1956 to today. I thank them for the unique experience afforded me, and curse them for their lack of compassion towards those who suffered from the aftermath of that experience.

For those readers who are unaware of some of the darker times, i.e. the 'Cold War' period of our 20th century history. This was a time when the Soviet Union and the Western Allies were approaching a nuclear standoff and the world was facing nuclear annihilation. During September and October 1956, the UK government held a series of four Atomic weapons tests at Maralinga in the south Australian desert. This Atomic weapons test site was purpose built with the agreement of the Australian federal government of that time, on the lands of the Maralinga Aboriginal Tjarutja people. Maralinga was a complete contrast to my other worldly travels. It is a very hot, dry place, in the middle of an arid, unforgiving red-sanded desert and 'bush'. It was said when we arrived there that, according to the local Aboriginal people it had not rained in the area for 50 years.

At the time, I was a 22-year-old Corporal Armament Fitter in the Royal Air Force, and five years into an eight-year engagement when I volunteered to take part in these weapons tests. I was one of the ground crew on 76 Squadron; our aircrews had the task of flying their aircraft through the resultant clouds from the detonations to take samples, a highly dangerous operation. Unwittingly on the ground, my colleagues and I would play a more intimate part in these 'spectaculars' than we might perhaps have wished; that is, had anyone bothered to explain to us the actions we would be required to do. I knew nothing about atomic weapons, but as an Armourer, weapons were my thing, and any chance to expand my experience was music to my ears. At the time I volunteered, or when finally posted to join the team, there was no information as to my duties, other than that everything was top secret.
It certainly expanded my experience!

I had no knowledge about the dangers of radiation exposure. I sincerely believe that had I known about the possibility of such dangers, I would still have wanted to go. Many of my colleagues received first-hand experience of those extreme dangers; some are still battling cancers etc. as result of involvement in those tests. Many more did not make it through to this time. The British government has taken the stance that they have no liability to the veterans from this period. Despite evidence to the contrary, they maintain their position.

This is in direct opposition to other nuclear nations who have stepped up to the plate and admitted that their tests may have caused injury and illness to the participants; subsequently they provided care and paid compensation.

Is the British government telling us that somehow or other, all the British tests were 'clean' and non-detrimental? Logic tells one that cannot be true.

Meanwhile, as the British Nuclear Test Veterans, campaign, watch and wait, the British government watches, waits also, then delays; they know that all they have to do is outwait the veterans for a few more years. The number of veterans from that distant time is decreasing rapidly, in a few years we will all be dead.

Problem solved for the government!

Not quite! The veteran's dependents are also campaigning, watching and waiting for recognition.

Chapter 1: Me, *versus* the RAF

Way, way back in 1955, whilst serving at Royal Air Force establishment, 32 Maintenance Unit, St. Athan, (for the uninitiated, that is in South Wales) I was a desperate individual seeking to escape from the monotonous confines of the said establishment. To say that I hated the place - would be a fair comment. It was a miserable existence, almost reminiscent of a basic training unit, but I loved my job there as an Armourer!

So how did I get there in the first place? The answer may seem simple to some, but to me it was a nasty shock, and not only culturally.

Up until April 1954, I had been enjoying a couple of years of an exciting, yet blissful life; living the open-air life of an Armourer in the Bomb Dump at RAF Seletar, Singapore. Part of that life included swanning around the Far East on Bomb Disposal duties amongst other things. I had been having such a good time that I had forgotten one simple fact, not all RAF life was on a par with that at RAF Seletar on Singapore Island.

This was at a time when the remnants of the old colonial ways of life were still around. For a naive 18-year-old kid it was somewhat embarrassing to have the locals who worked for us as labourers, and who were often two or three times my age, calling me 'Sir' or' Sahib'. As I came to know them better, I convinced them all they should just call me 'Simpson', or, as in the case of one of the general labourers, 'Soo Chow' an old Chinese man, – 'Shim-Shim'. His pronunciation was best that he could do around the solitary one tooth remaining in his mouth at the front of his top gum, the rest of his teeth were missing courtesy of a series of beatings by his Japanese captors during the occupation of Singapore from 1942 to 1945. For some reason he took a shine to me, watching my every move and shuffling in to help with whatever I was doing. When he knew I would be leaving to return to the UK, he asked me to marry his daughter and take her to the UK with me. That however, is another story for another day.

Being very young and naive, I was eagerly looking ahead to promotion as part of my career. First, though I would have to undergo advanced armament training to be eligible for promotion. In my naivety, I went against the advice from wiser heads regarding the logic of choosing the informality and ease of 'on the job' training at Seletar, or enduring all the 'bullshit and aggravation' of a training establishment which said establishment would incur. It is a fact, that the choices we make at various points in our lives determine the next direction in which our lives move. I was aware that 'on the job training,' would produce the same result as a training establishment. There was considerable pressure from all my superiors, right up to and including the Armament Officer for me to stay and do 'on the job' training. For some reason I assumed that doing a six-month course at a training establishment would give me more in depth knowledge and training.

Un-swayed, in early 1954 I requested a posting to RAF Kirkham in the UK so that I could take an Armament Fitters course; and was duly posted thereto. This entailed a 31-day 'cruise' back to the UK on board HMT Empire Trooper; arriving at Southampton just four days before the course commenced, missing the normal 14 days disembarkation leave. The detail of my successful culmination of the next six months existence and promotion to the rank of Junior Technician is not relevant here; suffice to say that there were times when I wished I had undertaken the offer of 'on the job' training so that I could still have been in Singapore!

Just prior to the completion of the course, I had the usual option at that time of making three choices of posting. Realising my original mistake when I elected for a course at a proper training school, against taking a local trade test at RAF Seletar where I could have continued to enjoy the good overseas life, I made my requests. My order of priority was FEAF, MEAF, and lastly Germany; my immature reasoning was, if I could not get back to the Far East then surely I'd get to the Middle East, if that failed then at the worst I'd get to Germany. Oh, the naivety of the young!

However, it would not work out quite like that; the RAF did not operate at my level of logic.
I'm sure that when my list of requests got to wherever it went within the system, mine was picked up by a vindictively bitter and twisted National Serviceman, who when he looked at where I'd been previously and where I wanted to go, decided to vent his frustration at being called up for National Service upon me. He probably said to himself, 'So he wants to go overseas again does he? Well let's see how he likes this; they need some Armament 'bods' at 32MU RAF St. Athan, in South Wales, that's as near to overseas as he's likely to get for a while!'
I was blissfully unaware of where my posting would be, but fully anticipated it would be overseas. In late October 1954 I successfully completed my course; gaining promotion to the rank of Junior Technician in the process. To my horror and dismay, I learned I was bound for 32MU RAF St. Athan. During the period of my course, I had heard so many tales of the miseries of life at 32MU; I was not looking forward to the posting. Whatever possessed me in not listening to my superiors in Singapore? How could I escape from this dreadful place and get back to the real world; or, was this the real world?

For the last 12 months, since I had been promoted to the rank of Corporal, I had been periodically evading my 'captors' by successfully applying for virtually every suitable detachment; even to as low as escorting a prisoner (one of my work colleagues) to the

Reg Simpson

Military Prison at Colchester. The highlight detachment had been a 30-day detachment to RAF Alhorn, Germany for Exercise Carte Blanche.

This was the first simulated nuclear war exercise of the Cold War. We joined the resident Meteor fighter squadron, who did not appear to know what to do with about thirty extra personnel. After spending a few days at RAF Alhorn, we then set off in a convoy of 15 trucks for a long road journey to RNAF Soesterberg, Holland. It was on the truck journey from Alhorn to Soesterberg that I experienced my most memorable meal. The day started with a wakeup call at 03.30hrs, breakfast at 04.00hrs and on the transport ready to leave at 04.30hrs. We made a stop at 08.00hrs for a hedgerow toilet break, a cup of tea and a curly sandwich (courtesy of Alhorn cookhouse) at the side of a road somewhere in Germany. The next stop was about noon, soon after we passed through Apeldoorn in Holland and into the countryside. A field kitchen was already set up, literally in the field; after a short delay, we filed along the front of the servery table to collect our food, some kind of tasty meat soup, a doorstep thick corn beef sandwich and a mug of tea. I have never been one for 'gourmet' food, for that matter, I am not sure what it really is. On that day, that meal has for whatever reason stayed in my memory. Simple fare, it may well have been, but everything tasted fantastic, to my simple mind, money could not have bought any better; nothing has matched it since. Sitting on the grass in the sunshine and peaceful countryside eating that meal felt so good.

I had not lost sight of the fact that only 11 years previously, where I was sitting, lives were being lost as the Allies pushed the Germans back towards Berlin. Field kitchen food would be the norm for the next two weeks, something which does not normally merit writing home about.

We arrived at RNAF Soesterberg in the late afternoon, before we could have a meal we had to unload the truckloads of equipment for our aircraft.

On day one of the exercise we had dig a series of slit trenches for ourselves. On day two, an umpire - a Dutch Army Major - came cycling round to tell us that we were all dead, killed by a Russian nuclear strike, and so could no longer take part. It was reminiscent of WW2 when the German Officer tells the Allied captives, 'For you the war is over'!

Not for us though the confines of a POW camp! The nearest comparison to that would be the terrible memories of sleeping on a Safari bed. For those who do not know, it is a very unforgiving concoction of, steel rods, plastic connectors and a canvas sling. A very uncomfortable piece of sleeping equipment, added to which we were living under canvas in a pine forest on the edge of the airfield, where we, all our kit and bedding was covered in black dust and dirt. The black dirt got in everywhere. Field showers (one short duration splash – one per day) are not a lot of help in keeping us clean. We spent each day for the next two weeks in a slit trench on the side of a small hill overlooking sun-drenched airfield at Soesterberg, drinking Heineken beer with our Dutch colleagues, before heading back to RAF Alhorn in Germany and then RAF St. Athan. Those Royal Nederland Air Force people had life well organised; whereas, in the UK we had the NAAFI van with tea and wads, the Dutch variety also carried beer – very civilised!

In addition to the above detachment to RAF Alcorn, throughout the 18 months at St Athan, I had made three abortive requests for postings to different units. I had also managed to get myself on a weeks' holiday to Blackpool – sorry, I mean an advanced 30mm Aden Gun course at RAF Kirkham. Next, was a non-existent

Reg Simpson

course at Martin Baker Aircraft Company. Getting my Section Officer's signature on the application for Martin Bakers was the usual doddle; he said it was a good idea, seeing as I was at that time in charge of the Ejection Seat service bay.

When I had to report to the Station Orderly Room, the Sergeant in charge was a different matter, he was nobody's fool. He insisted that as the course was not on his list, it did not exist. I did not know they even had a list! He was correct, but I insisted that a friend of mine in Bomber Command had just been on one (just a little white lie), so it was obviously a new course. Reluctantly he said he would forward my application onto Command Headquarters and we would find out in due course. Exactly one week later, I find that I am to be detached to RAF Ruislip to attend a five-day Martin Baker Ejection Seat course at the manufacturer's works at Denham, Bucks.

With 'the' famous Benny Lynch as my mentor (he, as of first man to make a live ejection from an aircraft), an enjoyable time ensued, including the lunchtime drinking with Benny at the Denham Lodge. The Sergeant was right, the course did not exist, but someone must have thought it was a good idea and hey presto!

Chapter 2: An Escape Route?

Returning from a spell of leave in early December 1955, I made tracks for the Daily Orders notice board outside the section office; not a detachment in sight! Just as I was moving away, one of the clerks arrived and pinned something on the board; he turned to me and said, "Here's one for you!"

I looked at the new notice, it read; **'VOLUNTEERS required for ATOMIC WEAPONS TRIALS, Maralinga, South Australia.'** I quickly perused the content; one of the trades required was Armament. That was good enough for me. As I pushed the office door open, the same clerk stood up and handed me an application form saying, "Sgt. Adams said, as soon as Cpl. Simpson sees that Order, he will be in to apply; so get an application form ready!"

Within a few minutes, I had completed the application and handed it to my section officer for his signature. He took the form and casually glancing at it said, "Another one? Where to this time? Oh! Australia, that's different!" With his signature appended, I gave the form back to the clerk.

Later during morning, I learned that I had to report to the Squadron Commander office at 14.00hrs that afternoon. I had been in the service long enough to recognise that interviews with the higher echelons get more serious with their increase in rank. Why did he want to see me I wondered? I know that having two stripes on your arm gave one a certain advantage in manipulating the system, a facility of which I made use of frequently. To my knowledge I had not overstepped the boundaries too far or been caught out in anything, I would have to wait until after lunch and find out.

As I waited in the Squadron Offices to see the Squadron Commander I racked my brains but could find no answer, why would he want to see me? I began to feel uncomfortably guilty for no particular reason. Could it be that …? No, that had happened nearly two months ago now. It is strange how in times of crisis, one can recall all the things you have done, that you should not have! As I stood to attention in front of the Squadron Commander, one Squadron Leader Murphy, commonly known to us all as 'Pat' because of his very heavy Irish accent, he said, "Stand easy Corporal".

Thank God! It was a signal that whatever it was, it was not serious; senior officers do not tell you to 'stand easy' when you are up to your neck in the proverbial.

He looked at me over the top of his glasses, waving my application and said, "I'm intrigued; all this Atomic weapons stuff might be dangerous. Do you know what it is all about?"

"No Sir, it sounds interesting and I'd like the opportunity to find out."

I could not tell him how desperate I was to get away from RAF St. Athan and 32 MU in particular. That sort of thing does not go down well with senior officers.

"OK, I'll approve your application and send it on; you will hear the result in due course. Dismiss!"

The next afternoon, I received instructions that I should report at 10.00hrs the following day to Warrant Officer Jones the Station Warrant Officer, to see the Station Commander, Group Captain Seymour. This made me more than a little nervous, usually we mere underlings would never be summoned to the 'top man's' presence, unless you were really in the mire. It was an anxious overnight wait, not improved by my colleagues, who could think of numerous possible and fictitious suggestions as to why the Group Captain would want to see me.

It is not particularly comforting to have friends around with a warped sense of humour in troubled times!

Dressed in my Best Dress uniform I cautiously knocked on the

SWO's door. This was the door of arguably the most powerful man at 32 MU RAF St. Athan; historically, he was one you trod lightly around; eventually the door opened, and he looked out.

"Oh! I see, so it is **that** Cpl. Simpson. Wait by my desk and I'll be back in a minute."

When he returned holding a brown file, I dutifully stood to attention in front of the desk. He looked me up and down critically. "Glad to see you're looking smart this morning. Do you know why the CO wants to see you? No? That's good!"

"Is there some sort of trouble Sir?"

"Trouble, why should there be trouble? What have you been up to? You haven't been in my flowerbeds again, have you?"

"No Sir!"

The 'flowerbeds' was a reference to the island garden in front of Station Headquarters.

A few weeks earlier, it had been my turn to march the armament section lads (120 of them in columns of three) from the billets to the workshop. It was a typical St. Athan foggy morning – could not see more than a few feet in front of you, let alone the front of a column forty men long. We always had problems with the 'Snowdrops' as we passed the Main Guardroom situated to the left of the island; they would nit-pick the lads as they marched (sic). I had told the lads at the head of the column to listen for my commands only and ignore the Snowdrops. We successfully (I was totally blind and working on a mental picture of our route) negotiated the first couple of turnings before the guardroom.

"Left Wheel, and ignore the Snowdrops," I bawled, in my best parade ground voice. Working from my mental picture of the route, I calculated it was about twenty paces before another 'left wheel' down the other side of the Guardroom. Before I could give the command, there was an almighty babble of voices from the head of the column and everyone stumbled to a halt. I raced to the front to find the first three rows of the lads were standing in the centre flowerbed; a Sgt. 'Snowdrop' and two of his minions were standing close by observing and seemingly lost for words for once. The SWO arrived on the scene; he was irate to say the least and wanted to know who was in charge. I owned up, as there was no other way out.

"What's your name Corporal and what section are you from?"

"Simpson, Sir! Armament Repair Section, Sir!"

"I will remember you for the future! Who gave you permission to trample my flowerbed with your clod-hopping armourers."?

"No one, Sir! I'm sorry, but it's difficult to see anything in this fog," I replied weakly.

"Excuses! Excuses! You people always have an excuse. Get this rabble out of my flowerbed. Get them to work, then report back to my office with these three idiots." He indicated the lads in the first row who were now trying to stifle their giggles. I formed the column up again and we proceeded down to the workshops. With the three lads in tow as we made our way back to report as directed, I asked them why they had not avoided the flowerbed. Their answer was that they were waiting for my command to turn; they did not hear anything so kept going straight on.

Oh, yes! Very funny indeed!

The SWO had us dig and repair the flowerbed; sadly, many of his pansies or whatever they were looked to be beyond recovery, so we just stuck them back in the ground with as many leaves showing as possible so they did not look too bad. When he came to inspect our handiwork, he took the opportunity to bawl the lads out for not using their heads and staying on the road.

I had hoped that time might have been a healer and he would have forgotten me, but apparently not.

"Have you been up in front of the 'CO' before Corporal?"

"No Sir."

"How have you managed that I wonder?"

I made no comment.

"I'll march you in and you will stand to attention in front of his desk, and then salute."

As I was marched in I was still wondering what I might have done. I stood stiffly at attention and saluted.

The SWO spoke, "Corporal Simpson as requested Sir."

The CO nodded.

"The gardener, Sir!" the SWO added sarcastically.

"OK Mr. Jones that will be all. I will call you." The SWO marched out.

The CO cleared his throat, "You do know Corporal that those gardens are Mr. Jones' pride and joy?"

"So it would appear sir, but it was a very foggy morning. Is this why I am here sir?"

"No, and you can stand easy now."

It could not be too bad if I could 'stand easy'.

"I have here your application for a posting to Australia for the upcoming Atomic Weapons Trials."

I relaxed; I should have realised it was my application, and nothing more. Did I have a guilt complex?

He continued on, "You do realise that you may be exposed to atomic radiation which is dangerous, and could harm you for life? This area of weaponry is very much in the early stages of development. Do you know anything at all about Atomic bombs?"

"No sir, I only know that they were used by the Americans on Hiroshima and Nagasaki in 1945."

"That is what worries me; there has been a great deal of residual illness and effects for the Japanese people from that time. Why do you want to take part in these trials?"

I really did not know, other than it was a way of escape from his Station and I could not tell him that. Therefore, I reverted to my line that the trials were a way of moving into future weaponry and it would be interesting to be a part of the project.

"Well if you are sure you really want to go I'll approve your request with a strong recommendation that it is accepted. By the way, how do you like being stationed at RAF St. Athan?"

Had he heard something? Guilt again?

I took my courage in both hands, "I don't sir."

"Well, maybe this will rectify the situation for you. Good luck"

I thanked him. He pressed a button on his desk; the SWO appeared alongside me and marched me out of the office. Outside in the corridor the SWO dismissed me and told me to stay clear of his gardens.

As I walked down to the hangar where I worked, I mused over the interview. Would I be lucky, and be selected for this posting? What then, would I be working with atomic bombs? What exactly would I be doing? My mind boggled with the possibilities. Like most things in the services, what you get, is not always what you are expecting.

A few days before Christmas 1955, I received notice that w.e.f. Wednesday 18th April 1956 I was to be posted to 160 Wing Detachment at RAF Weston Zoyland, to join 76 Squadron on 'OPERATION BUFFALO' prior to deploying to the Maralinga Atomic Weapons Test site in Australia. Although it was more than three months hence, I was over the moon, but there was a slight problem. I had recently met a very special girl who was tugging my heartstrings. Why is life's path not a smooth one? That however, is another story.

A couple of days prior to my posting I embarked on that most joyous of occasions; going around the station getting my clearance 'chit' signed off by the various departments. When I handed my completed chit back in, the Orderly Room Sergeant took me into another room and told me to wait there. An Officer entered the room looking at some papers in his hand, he asked me for my Number, Rank and Name, I tell him, and he hands me my rail travel and movement documents. Then he tells me that I should not discuss 'Operation Buffalo' with anyone; what I do and where I am going to is Top Secret. I must not discuss it with anyone, not even my family. He produced a document for me to sign. All I remember about it was that the heading read 'Official Secrets Act'. I would be travelling to RAF Weston Zoyland with one other person from the unit, another Corporal. He, I found out, was an Instrument 'wallah'; that was not his fault, not everyone could be an Armourer!

I could hardly believe my luck, I had achieved what I had become to think was bordering on the impossible; namely to escape from 32MU St Athan. I had no idea, that all my previously vain attempts to get away from St Athan would culminate in my having the experience of a lifetime at Maralinga.

Reg Simpson

Chapter 3: The Start of an Experience.

The next morning, dressed in our 'best blues', my colleague and I meet up on the railway platform at St. Athan Halt, and travelled together to Bridgewater. From there we travelled by bus to the village of Weston Zoyland; arriving there, we stood at the bus stop not knowing which way to go. No one had said if there would be any transport to collect us. My colleague suggested that we ask the woman coming towards us, if she knew the way to the camp. We did not need to ask, she spoke first in a thick Somerset accent.

"Be yuse lookin' fur t' Camp?"

I said we were, and asked how far it was.

Ignoring my question she said, "Yuse be gwine to Orstrailier on that Buffalo thingy then?"

Mindful of the warning about secrecy, we looked at each other and burst out laughing.

"Whatever's that?" I asked.

"Oh, it be Top Secret an' all that. They Ministry people, they don't want nobody t' know 'bout it, so we don't talk about it. T' camps down thur, round t' bend, down t' lane on yur left and then on a tad. Oi'd show yuse, but oi'm gwine tuther way. They sez they gits plenty o' sunshine in Orstrailier!"

Top Secret operation???? Some secret! Maybe I should have asked her what it was that I would be doing.

Hardly able to contain our laughter, we thanked her and went off in the direction given. Finding the lane, we walked on, humping our kitbags from one shoulder to the other in the warm sunshine. It seemed a long way before we saw the camp gate and the guardroom. The 'Snowdrops' were their usual helpful selves, one telling us that we should have waited at the bus stop for the transport that ran every hour. He indicated the pickup truck that was just going out through the gate. Some help that was!

Reg Simpson

"Orderly Room? Straight on until you see the sign," he said.
At the Orderly Room, we are greeted by a Cpl. who introduced himself as Mick Foran, as Irish as they come he said. "Lunch finished an hour ago, so dump your gear in the corner there and I'll get the cookhouse to rustle up something to eat."

I don't know why, but every time I arrived on a new unit, for whatever reason, I always arrived after the cookhouse had closed. This was the first time someone had made a special effort for me to eat; usually I had to wait until the next mealtime. 'Mick' took us to the cookhouse where the cook made us some bacon and eggs followed by tinned pears. Back at the Orderly Room we were told that we would be joining 76 Sqdn. Mick delegated one of his clerks to take us to our accommodation and then to 76 Sqdn offices.
At the Squadron offices, we reported to the Flight Sergeant who welcomed us to Bomber Command and 76 Sqdn detachment. He said that 76 Sqdn would be flying three Canberra B6's, on cloud sampling duties. As the aircraft had not yet arrived, he said we should hang around in the crew room, and keep a low profile for a few days until they turned up. The delay was due to something to do with last minute modifications to the equipment.

The next day another Armourer, SAC Tom Heenan, joined me, we would be working together, or as he put it, he would be my right hand man, so long as I when I went to the toilet I was left-handed! I now had my own section with a staff of one! The aircraft arrived one at a time over the next week. Therefore, we had little to do except keep a low profile to ensure we were not 'volunteered' for anything.
When our Canberra B6 bombers did turn up, I was surprised that they had no bomb gear in the bomb bay. Instead, hung on the main bomb release unit was a large cylindrical unit with domed ends, with pipes running from it into the fuselage. The unit filled the total

space in the bomb bay. We obviously were not going to drop any bombs with these aircraft! We learned that 'cloud sampling' was done by the aircrew flying the aircraft through the resultant cloud from the bomb. That sounded a bit hairy for the crews! We did not know just how dangerous that would turn out to be until later! The equipment on board would take in the air and particles into the tank suspended in the bomb bay via the pods on the wingtips, which also had filters to collect 'debris' samples.

The next few weeks were spent familiarising ourselves with the aircraft, I had worked on Canberra B2s previously at St Athan so was basically familiar with the aircraft except for a few upgrades. Life was easy going at Weston Zoyland, Tom and I found it easy to avoid getting detailed for the occasional parade that took place. We only worked Monday to Friday, so each weekend I could go home for a couple of days. I was going to be away for a year, so every day that I could get home made it easier to deal with my love affair, or so I thought! It must have done, because we became engaged in May, hoping to marry in October 1957

In addition to our familiarisation period with the aircraft, there were other events taking place at the same time. We all had medicals, chest X-rays, blood tests, and the inevitable inoculations before going overseas. The 'jab' sessions were always good for a laugh; you would form the inevitable queue and shuffle forward to the 'needle point'. I would always be listening for the sound as the occasional body slumped to the floor. Usually it was someone ahead of you in the queue but occasionally it would be behind you as nerves got the better of someone. To break the tedium of the wait of the line I used to try to spot a likely fainter, would it be the big 'macho' bloke or one of the 'mummy's boys'.
There were security sessions, where we filled out security clearance forms; those of us on 76 Sqdn that would be going to the forward

area i.e. Maralinga had to complete an 'in depth security clearance' form, known as 'Positive Vetting'. That consisted of repeating on the form, that information which we had put on the basic security clearance form. In addition, several new questions plus having to nominate two character referees. For my referees I nominated a farmer friend with whom I had grown up, and another farmer who knew me who was also, a Justice of the Peace. When you come from a 'country bumkin' background, it is hard to know who knows you well enough, for you to nominate them as a referee, we did not live that kind of life.

A few weeks later when I was at home at the weekend, I went to visit my farmer friend. He wanted to know what I had been up to, because he had had two men in bowler hats and as he called them, city suits, turn up at the farm the week previously asking questions about me. I asked what sort of questions they were; he said they wanted to know if, I had any political interests, had I ever been in trouble with the police and was I trustworthy. If that was positive vetting, then they must have been satisfied.
Finally, we were issued with our tropical kit; this, they said we would need as the Australian desert gets very hot. We were now approaching our departure date and would be flying from Stanstead Airport in a RAF transport Command aircraft.

We were two weeks from departure when there was a 'panic' on. Apparently, one of the RAF Transport Command aircraft of the same type as we were due to fly on via the Middle East, had crashed on landing somewhere. Consequently, all aircraft of that type had been grounded. Those of us headed for Maralinga were required to be in Australia ASAP, the Air Ministry had to make alternative arrangements and had booked all the available seats with BOAC. There was now a panic to get us passports, and an urgent session of photos and completing of passport applications ensued. My occupation was 'Government Official' instead of an obscure RAF bod. Within three days, our passports were issued to us. I had never had a passport before; looking at the first page, I was impressed to see my occupation listed 'Government Official'. It was a bit of an ego boost to think I was 'someone' more than just a Number, Rank and Name!! During the same session, we were reminded that we were bound by the Official Secrets Act that we had recently signed, contravention of which would incur severe penalties. We were instructed, to travel in civilian clothes and not to disclose or indicate that we were RAF personnel. We should also obtain from a bank the maximum sum of ten US dollars for pocket money in the United States. For later flights, I understand that the Pay Accounts Section made US dollars available which was a much better idea. We would be flying out to Australia via the States.

That weekend on the Saturday morning, whilst home, I went into Lloyds Bank, Above Bar Branch, in Southampton to get my dollars. I was in for an enlightening experience with a touch of snobbery. Foreign currency for the public was difficult to get, it was strictly controlled and in short supply. The country was in effect still broke, having not recovered from the war.
I waited my turn, and asked the clerk for ten US dollars. He said that I could not have any due to restrictions imposed by the Bank of England. I told him I had been instructed by the Air Ministry to get some dollars. After a bit of a standoff he went to get the Chief Clerk, who repeated his junior's statement. I repeated mine.
"How many do you want," he asked frostily.
"Ten please."
"Most unlikely, have you got your passport?"
I handed it over.
"I'll have to check with the Branch Manager."
He disappeared through a doorway, and was quickly back; now all

smiles.

"The Manager would like to see you; if you would come this way."
I was ushered into a rather palatial office and the presence of the
Manager, who seemed to leap to his feet and reached over the desk
to shake my hand.

"Mr. Simpson, I'm sorry, but we had no idea that you were a
Government Official. You should have said who you were."
I said there was no need to apologise. I could afford to be
magnanimous seeing as how he thought I was more important than
I was.

"Are you sure that you only need ten dollars? There is no limit for
people like you on official business."

"Yes, all I need is ten. Could I have them in one-dollar bills,
please?"
I did not think it wise to enlighten him that I could only afford to
buy ten dollars. The exchange at the time was about four dollars to
the pound sterling. The Chief Clerk went out returning with my ten
dollars and I signed the receipt in exchange for my two pounds and
odd change. The Manager escorted me back out to the foyer, as he
shook my hand he offered his services at any time. Maybe he
thought that I might hold some influence in the next Honours List!
As I walked back round the corner to the Bus station, I realised that
having a passport showing I was a Government Official could be a
major asset. How I wondered, could I take advantage of it? It
would not be until several years later, in Majorca, as it transpired.

This was to be my last weekend at home; we were due to fly out the
next week. It was not a traumatic weekend as such, probably a bit
of sweet and sour. Up until the last Christmas the RAF had been at
the centre of my life, everything else was secondary. Fortunately,
the girl who had entered my life since that time understood my
priorities – I think! I like to think that she was proud of me being in
the RAF. She was from a military related family, albeit on the

Royal Navy side.

When she was only three years old, her father was in the Royal Naval Volunteer Reserve and killed, (missing in action presumed killed) in the sinking of the battleship HMS Hood on 24th May 1941. Like many families during the 1939-1945 conflict, she and her mother also had the first-hand experience of being on the end of bombing raids by the enemy, and of having to grow up without a husband and father.

Her mother on the other hand, was understandably extremely bitter about losing her husband. She previously had told me that she was not too happy about her daughter's husband being in the Armed Forces', and the possibility of her also becoming a widow. I tried to allay her fears by explaining that the likelihood of my getting killed was remote; RAF ground crew were most unlikely ever to come face to face with the enemy. How do you delicately tell a war widow that kind of thing, when they know that the odds are always there? It is no point in pretending to others that the odds did not exist, she probably knew this better at than me. The trauma of loss for her had been even greater, when her husband's younger brother also in the navy, was a victim of the enemy at sea, only two months before her own loss. With the death of the brother in law in February 1941, there is no doubt that the event would have heightened her fears for her husband, and her bitterness is fully understandable. The loss of her husband ruined the rest of her life and she naturally did not want her daughter to experience the same.

Over these latter months, I had had to reconsider my priorities; back in May - the 19th - so I am reliably informed - we had become engaged, with a target date of marriage soon after when I returned in a year's time. Now, my life had taken on a bit of turmoil, I had two loves. One I would have to leave behind, whilst I indulged in the other! I was committed to going to Australia by my service duty, and I personally wanted to go. On the other hand, I did not

want to leave my bride to be! What would have happened if I could have had a choice of going to Australia or staying at home? Fortunately, I never had to find out; it might have been too devastating.
Goodbyes said, I returned to Weston Zoyland.

Now back in camp, our airline tickets were issued to us; our departure date was Thursday 26th July. We knew that due to the urgency of the situation to get us to Australia, we had been booked on to the first available flights. What we had no idea of, was the itinerary, so it was a pleasant surprise to see how our group were booked:
Heathrow to New York (Idlewild – now JFK) on BOAC *Majestic Class. (First Class) Flight No: BA 515,* Aircraft – Stratocruiser, Via -**Manchester, Prestwick, Reykjavik, Thule, Gander and New York.**

New York to San Francisco – on United Airlines - *First Class.* Aircraft – DC6
Overnight at Clift Hotel, San Francisco (5 Star)

San Francisco to Sydney (Kingsford Smith) on Qantas – *Economy Class.* Aircraft – Super Constellation.
Via – **Honolulu, Canton, Fiji and Sydney.**

Sydney to Adelaide – Australian National Airlines – **Economy Class**. Aircraft – Unknown, it was most probably a turbo-propeller engine aircraft, or as we used to call them – 'Paddles and Elastic bands'.

Chapter 4: Outbound to South Australia.

Thursday 26th July 1956, it was a sunny day as we boarded two RAF coaches for Heathrow airport and set off on our journey. A party atmosphere prevailed on our bus with much joviality, singing of raucous songs and ditties. We stopped for a noonday refreshment break at a pub near Basingstoke. Lolling around on the grass in the sunshine outside the pub, supping our pints and chewing on corned beef sandwiches (courtesy of the Weston Zoyland cookhouse – sandwiches, not beer) was reminiscent of my younger days when on the Botley British Legion's day out at the seaside. Back then, we always stopped somewhere short of the destination for a few beers from the many crates carried in the luggage storage under the coach.

Lunch over we continued on to Heathrow airport where we were dropped off outside a corrugated iron clad building, totally unrecognisable in comparison to the airport of today. At the check-in desk, a man checked my ticket and gave me a boarding card with a seat number on it, my number was C36. We climbed aboard a bus, which took us out to the aircraft, a Boeing Stratocruiser with its distinctive figure '8' fuselage. As I entered the aircraft door a very pleasant and attractive Air Hostess' with an accent that my mother would have described as 'posh', welcomed me on board, on behalf of BOAC. Looking at my ticket, she addressed me as Mr. Simpson and showed me to my seat, making sure I understood how it operated. It was more like a reclining armchair than a seat! In no time it seemed, we were roaring down the runway and airborne. There was a short hop to Manchester, where we picked up a few Americans judging by their accents. Then another short hop, to Prestwick; where four more Americans boarded. Next stop, after an in-flight meal was Reykjavik in Iceland, another 6 American service members and some fuel. Back in the air, a full meal this time, the next stop was Thule in Greenland, where four American army officers boarded. There was a large American radar station at Thule. With fuel topped up again, the next stop was at Gander in New Foundland, here we could get off the plane, but there was nowhere to go, it was a desolate place, cold and windy. We loaded more fuel, re-boarded and were ready for take-off. Once airborne there was more food, I cannot remember what it was. Now we were on the final leg to Idlewild (now JFK) New York, where we landed in a violent thunderstorm. It was an extremely rough approach to our landing, and it really aggravated my motion sickness. Throughout the flight, there had been a constant flow of drinks, snacks and meals. How I managed to hang onto the contents of my full stomach, was nothing short of a miracle. It was with considerable relief when I stepped onto terra firma again and the world stopped doing an Irish jig. Motion sickness apart, if my experience on this flight was anything to judge by, then travelling First Class was without doubt, the way to go.

When we went through the immigration control, I handed my passport and ticket to the inspector, he flipped them open, as he handed them back to me he said, "Looks as if the whole British Government is moving out to Australia. You people know something we don't? Have a good trip!"
There followed a boring 3 ½ hour wait until our next flight departed to San Francisco, there wasn't much to do to pass the time. I had an interesting experience whilst waiting, one of the many vending machines was one that sold drinks, and one of the drinks listed was Root Beer. I had no idea what this was, but it had the word beer in the name, so that would be all right? How wrong can one be? It tasted vile, and ever since then in my travels around the United States of America, I have steered clear of Root Beer. Yuck!

I was extremely happy when it was time to board our flight on the next leg. Shortly after take-off, again travelling first class, a large tempting glass of orange juice finally cleared that vile taste of Root Beer, from my mouth. I wondered if United Airlines 'First Class' would be similar to BOAC's, in short it was not.

It was about 6 PM when we arrived in San Francisco and by 6:30 PM, we were at the hotel. The Clift Hotel was very impressive, I forget how many floors there were, but I do know that each floor was panelled out in a different wood. The floor I was on was known as the Redwood floor, with all the walls panelled in Redwood, very impressive. We were allocated rooms with two single beds, my roommate being an engine mechanic. It seemed to take us longer to check into the hotel and our allotted rooms, than it did to get from the airport to the hotel.

My roommate and I decided not to eat in the hotel but to have a look around the area near to the hotel. A short way from the Hotel was a place called a 'Diner'. We found ourselves a table and waited for service, the server as soon as she realised we were English, made us feel especially welcome. Before we could order anything, she went to the bar and brought back two ice-cold Budweiser beers on the house, and telling us that her mother came from England. The man and woman sitting at the next table had overheard the conversation and asked us to join them at their table. The man had arrived in England during the Second World War just before D-Day. They insisted on buying our meal and when we had finished they suggested that they take us for a ride around San Francisco to show us the sights. We had an enjoyable evening in their company, and when they dropped us back at the hotel it was nearly 10 o'clock and time for bed, as we had to be up in time to get some breakfast and to catch the bus, which would leave the hotel at 07.00 hrs. At 06.00hrs the next morning we crossed the road to the same diner, our server from the previous night was not on duty. We both ordered scrambled egg, bacon, toast and tea. The tea was a new experience for us, not made in the traditional way with loose tealeaves in a teapot, but from a bag of tealeaves on a string to dunk in the warm water, not hot water, much to the consternation of my colleague. He had a rather loud voice when talking and it seemed to reverberate around the diner. How he wanted to know, was it that these people did not know how to make tea, using near boiling water. A man sat on the next table behind him had the perfect answer. He said, 'You've got your castles and we've got our modern conveniences'. Fortunately, it was time for us to leave and get back to the hotel, so avoiding any possible diplomatic incident.

At the airport, we joined our Qantas flight to Sydney, the aircraft this time was a Lockheed Super Constellation, and we now had a downturn in our status to economy class, instead of first class. Our first stop would be Honolulu, followed by Canton, then Fiji and finally Sydney, with no overnight stops. Arriving at Honolulu the weather was lovely, it was warm, humid, and balmy; as we stepped onto the tarmac, girls in Hawaiian grass skirts hung a garland of flowers around our necks. Prior to disembarking, our flight attendants had suggested we did not get a meal whilst on the ground, we had a one-hour half-hour refuelling stop and as soon as we were airborne, we would be having a cooked meal. Therefore, naturally, we made a beeline for the open-air restaurant. The four of us at our table each had fillet steak and chips, followed in my case by a fruit salad, which was a pineapple sliced in half with all the centre scooped out and piled back in together with other fruits, of which I had never seen nor tasted before, or even knew what they were. It was a very pleasant experience.

All too soon, we had to climb the steps into the aircraft and move on to the next leg of our journey to the island of Canton.

Surprise! Surprise! Within the hour of being airborne, as promised, a steak meal appeared in front of us. The flight attendants were not too pleased because most of us could not manage to ram anymore down into our gorged guts. Somewhere between Honolulu and Canton, we crossed the equator. There was no traditional crossing of the line ceremony as is on board a ship; as the captain of the aircraft said, we were flying a little too high to dip anyone in the water.

When we arrived at Canton, we were much more circumspect and listened to the advice of the flight attendant's. There was little to see at Canton it was purely an aircraft refuelling point as a means to crossing the Pacific Ocean. The Americans had built it during the war for the convenience of their air force. Whilst the plane refuelled, we could disembark if we wished, and wait in the tiny little corrugated tin clad terminal building. It was a welcome opportunity to stretch our legs, and on a little coral island that is unheard of and never seen by todays flying public, to the extent that, I cannot find it on a map anymore. Soon we were airborne again and en route to Fiji, a place I knew little about, only that it used to have some beautiful postage stamps. Arriving at Fiji was not unlike as I remembered Singapore; many palm trees, beautifully warm weather, and a torrential rainstorm that was finished within 15 minutes. We had again been warned by the flight attendants not to eat whilst here on the ground, because they did not want a repeat of the last episode! I think in general, most of us complied with their suggestions this time, though we did visit the restaurant and have a couple of beers; and in my case, an ice cream followed by the beers. With the aircraft refuelled and some new passengers embarked, we took off for Sydney.

Shortly after take-off, the flight attendant came round and issued to every one of us a personalised 'crossing of the line' certificate, signed by the captain of the aircraft.

Whilst back in my troopship days I had crossed the 'line' a couple of times, once out, once back, I had never received a certificate That Quantas certificate is still one of my prized possessions. On the troopships, we did have the 'crossing the line' ceremonies, where several unfortunates were duly drenched in buckets of seawater and received a certificate for their efforts.

The journey from Fiji to Sydney I recall very little of, accept that every time I looked out the window there was nothing but water below. When we landed in Sydney (Kingsford Smith Airport), we changed airlines and aircraft for the journey onto Adelaide. The airline was Australian National Airlines and the type of aircraft eludes my memory.

Chapter 5: Welcome to South Australia.

At least on this journey we were flying over land all the time, for a short while after leaving Sydney the land was green with trees etc. Thereafter, the scenery changed to a brown coloured desert, then the weather deteriorated to heavy cloud and rain, the nearer we approached Adelaide the bumpier became the ride. Landing at Adelaide, the rain eased off as we walked from the aircraft to the terminal building. After finding our kitbags and exiting the terminal building, we climbed into the backs of several three-ton trucks for our journey to RAAF Edinburgh field.

A thought struck me when picking up my kitbag in the arrivals hall at Adelaide. If our journey was so secret, i.e. civilian clothes and no talk of RAF, or where or what we were doing etc., anyone with half a brain would have seen us for what we were, RAF personnel in civilian clothes humping kitbags with our number, rank and name splashed all over it; some secrecy!

It was an uneventful journey to RAAF Edinburgh Field, apart from the terribly bumpy road and uncomfortable seats in the back of trucks. The slatted wooden seats of the truck did little to stabilise one's body as you slid backwards and forwards on them. In addition, thrown bodily from side to side, and up and down by the machinations of the truck and driver. The driver, from the Aussie air force had all the signs and machinations of a frustrated 'wannabe racing driver', braking at the last moment before straightening the bend, then stamping on the accelerator, and not slowing down for the rougher sections of the road.

Perhaps he was also a frustrated pilot, because the truck seemed to spend more time in the air than it did on the ground. The journey was more than somewhat hair-raising, and I was not sorry when we pulled into Edinburgh field. As if to welcome us to Australia after our long journey, there was a steady cold drizzling rain. There was a growing train of thought amongst some of my colleagues, that the Aussies had organised the miserable weather and the truck journey especially for us as a welcoming present. We should have realised that it was winter now on this side of the world!

The accommodation was a unique surprise; the billets were in converted explosives storage buildings, complete with blast walls around them. Ours had been an explosives magazine and was instantly recognisable to me, having spent many days humping boxes of explosives and ammunition in and out of them in Singapore. They would prove to be reasonably cool in the summer and not too cold in the winter when the heating was on, as it was now. Having dumped our kit on our beds we set off to the bedding store to collect bedding.

Guess what? The moment we came out of the bedding store with our arms loaded with blankets etc., the heavens opened and the rain poured down. Trying to run as fast as possible with your arms loaded with bedding is not exactly easy, and to make matters worse several of us could not remember which of the identical buildings was ours. After two false attempts, I found the billet that I had been in and dumped the now very damp bundle onto the bedspring. As I sorted through the bundle I realised that for once, I had made a smart move, I had used one blanket, as a sling to carry the other stuff in fortunately, this was the only one that was too wet to put straight on the bed. I managed to get my blanket onto the nearest radiator where it would hopefully, dry out by bedtime.

Our surprises were not over yet, it was time to get over to the mess hall for a meal. As we lined up to be served, complementary comments began to drift back down the line from those at the front. Nearing the servery, the menu board was a revelation. There were five choices of meats, many vegetables, salads, and at least six choices of sweets (as in pudding), fresh and canned fruit, a multitude of cakes and pastries, coffee, tea, and a wide selection of soft drinks. It really was difficult making choices. The gluttons amongst us must have thought they had died and gone to a glutton's heaven. Whatever choice you made, the cook serving the food piled it on and then asked you if that was enough, also telling us that should we still be hungry, supper would be served between 20.00hrs and 22.00hrs. It was bewildering to someone coming from a still austere Britain, that there was such an excess of food.

I did have one complaint, once you sat at the table, you faced a bewildering multitude of condiments, vinegars, sauces, salad dressings, most of which I had never seen or heard of. For instance, salt; as far as I ever knew there was only one kind of salt, - white table salt. Where had I been all my life? Lined up on the table in front of us was, white table salt, sea salt, celery table salt, garlic table salt and a brown coloured salt that looked, smelled, and tasted vile. Why should I have complained with such a wide variety of choice? Answer, they were all in identical shakers, to the uninitiated they all looked the same. Needless to say, there were many ruined meals before we cottoned onto the fact that the tops were discreetly marked. The simple table manners request, 'Pass the salt, please', was fraught with danger. The unscrupulous amongst us would often switch the tops on the shakers, for instance, to deliver a dose of garlic to ruin someone's meal. Being as we were in the main, of non-Gallic or Roman descent, the disturbing taste and smell of a heavy dose of garlic for the rest of the night was a most unwelcome experience. It may not have been good table manners, but a precautionary sniff of the shaker top was always wise before giving the container a good shake!
I think it is fair to say in mitigation; the biter, was very often bitten.

We rounded off the first evening with a visit to the Aussie equivalent of the NAAFI; they called it the 'wet' and 'dry' canteens. The 'wet' was where you could buy beer, the 'dry' where you would buy all dry goods including food. Most of us gravitated to the wet canteen where we were in for another slight cultural shock. We Poms had always supped from pint glasses, straight or with a handle. There was little point in asking for a pint, the beer or lager in Aussie terms, came in a glass smaller than a pint, known as a schooner. That was not all, the schooner when served was filled with a mixture of lager and a large foaming head, resulting in the schooner containing three quarters lager and a quarter of foam. We soon adapted to this quaint colonial custom of short-changing. Having quaffed several schooners we headed back to our accommodation and bed. I was pleased to find that my blanket had dried out so that I could make up my bed properly. I slept very soundly that night. I could not believe it when my roommate was shaking my shoulder telling me it was time to get up or we would miss breakfast. Had those Aussies tampered with the lager?

Breakfast was yet another culinary experience, more choices. Canned and fresh fruit, several cereals - some familiar ones others never heard of, loads of fried bacon, eggs - fried, scrambled, poached, boiled; chips, sausages of varying descriptions, baked beans, fried bread and loads of toast, not to mention white bread, brown bread, other coloured breads, real butter, jams, honey, chocolate spread, to mention but a few! I don't think there was one of us who was not dumbfounded by the food culture shock. I personally had never seen such an array or quantity of food in my life. If only my family at home could have shared it, they would I am sure, have been gobsmacked! The UK was just emerging from the final restrictions of food rationing.

What a welcome to Australia the previous 18 hours had been, if our Aussie pals had organised it as a welcoming reception, they could not have done better!

Were our Aussie mates trying to show us their superiority in life, and not just in cricket?

Over the next year, particularly whilst at Maralinga, there would always be keen competition in most matters, between our Aussie compatriots and us. I believe that the culprit in this inevitable competitive spirit was the fault of the sport of cricket. Nationally over the years, Australia and England were bitter rivals to win the 'Ashes', the ultimate cricketing trophy.

Stuffed to the gills with food we raced back to the accommodation for a shave and shower to get ready for whatever the day may throw at us. For those of us who would be working at the airstrip, there was a short truck journey of about half a mile and we were there.

There was not a lot to do for the first week, as the Canberras had not arrived yet; hanging around in the hangar was boring. As soon as they did arrive, it was all hands to the deck to get the ground equipment ready to load up and shipped to Maralinga. The first week of August, those of us who were going on to Maralinga had to get our documentation and security passes for the Maralinga range area. There were also several more Official Secrets Act papers, Maralinga Range passes to complete and sign. The Squadron adjutant informed us that photography, was not permitted where we were going; therefore, our personal cameras were to be left in his care until we returned. Together with a couple of others, I rather reluctantly handed over my Leica camera for which I received a receipt telling me it would be stored in the Squadron adjutant's safe. One or two of the lads must 'not have heard him', because when we were at Maralinga they still had their cameras, and used them. I was a bit peeved about the camera, because I had only just recently purchased it from a cash-strapped Aussie armourer at a knockdown price, specifically to take to Maralinga. Well, orders are orders, so be it.

Reg Simpson

It was about mid-August when we were advised to pack our kit (blue uniforms etc.) other than the tropical kit, ready to be placed into storage for when we returned to Edinburgh field. The rest of our kit we packed into our kitbags, ready for the flight to Maralinga the following day. Since our arrival, the weather had improved considerably with more sunny warm days than cold wet days. I for one was looking forward to the promised hot weather in Maralinga, which was about 400 miles North West of Adelaide.

Chapter 6: Maralinga – Fields of Thunder

The aboriginal word 'Maralinga', translates as 'Fields of Thunder', which was very appropriate for what was to transpire there.

We arrived at Maralinga via, a very uncomfortable and bumpy flight in a Hastings aircraft; a four engine transport aircraft, from RAAF Edinburgh Field. We bundled aboard a 3-ton truck for the short bumpy ride, from the airstrip up to the Village, situated on top of the only hill in the area. No matter which way you looked, not another hill in sight, just lots of red sand and scrub, clear blue skies and a hot, dry wind. The welcoming party was a sole RAAF warrant officer. I thought he took considerable delight in breaking the news that, the RAF contingent (other ranks below Sgt.)living accommodation was not yet ready, due to the civilian contractors being way behind on their schedule.

In breaking the news about the accommodation to us, the welcoming Warrant Officer said we should not worry because we could sleep in the fire station, now they had moved the fire engines out. The first unwelcome sight was the concrete floor, rough finished and very dusty. The second was when the Warrant Officer indicated that we should get ourselves a bed from the stack in the corner of the building, my heart sank when I saw them. The beds were, in RAF parlance 'Beds - Safari', a concoction of metals rods, several plastic connectors and canvas sling contained in a canvas type bag; in my experience, these were very unstable and uncomfortable. It might be that when the plastic connectors were new they held the rods securely, but once they began to slacken due wear, a collapse was inevitable. That contraption brought back bad memories of uncomfortable nights and little sleep during 'Exercise Carte Blanche', a simulated nuclear attack by the Russians held in Holland during 1955. That episode is part of another story.

Reg Simpson

Maralinga was a desolate place with little entertainment facilities other than that which we made for ourselves; the place was after all, still rising out of the red desert sand. The only acknowledgement to civilisation was just the Aussie military's 'wet' and 'dry' canteens. There was no cinema or swimming pool as was to be in later 'operations'. About halfway through Buffalo some of us thought it was a good idea to turn the emergency fire water supply tank into a swimming pool. It seemed a good idea at the outset; the tank was about half the size of a swimming pool, it did not have a 5 m diving board, which was just as well! Most of us did not have swimming attire, as a swimming pool is not something you expect to find in the middle of the desert. So for most of us it was a case of 'skinny-dipping', and ignoring the no swimming notice attached of the tank.

After my first session in the tank, I noticed that I had a peculiar odour about me. Stagnant water has its own pungent odour and unselfishly shares it with anyone foolish enough to get in it. Even after showering, I was sure that I still had that peculiar smell attached, so decided that I would stick to having a shower as opposed to having a swim, that is, providing we still had the water pressure for the showers. Other more hardy souls continued with the makeshift swimming pool until someone in authority heard about it and banned the practice.

As there were no aircraft yet to work on and to keep us occupied and out of mischief, some bright spark found us work with the civilian contractors on various construction activities. I found myself working with a gang of four plumbers repairing water supply pipes in the roadway of the Village. As vehicular traffic went along the road, their weight broke the pipes buried beneath. It was easy to see why; underlying the sand of the road was uneven coral rock. The pipes, made of a fibrous cement substance, had unwisely (or otherwise), been laid directly onto the uneven coral. We worked on a junction of four roads near the fire station for three days. There were so many repairs made to some of the pipes, the only logical solution was to replace them, only to repair them again the following morning. That was nothing but a cyclic waste of time and money. Each morning you could see where the damaged pipes were. An obvious indicator was a damp patch of sand, a bubbling spring or often a four feet high geyser! It is no wonder that our showers often had little water pressure. On the third day, I suggested to the supervisor that a solution would be to place a layer of sand on top of the coral to cushion the pipes. My innocent suggestion did not go down very well at all with the civvies. It was then that I found out that they had been working on this junction for the past three weeks for 12 hours each day, seven days a week! They were not going to be amenable to any suggestions that might reduce their undemanding, money spinning opportunity. In my ignorance, I suggested that they might be ripping somebody off; they were not appreciative of my comments.

They did not send me to 'Coventry' exactly; let us say the conversations were noticeably restricted to the job in hand. The following morning, the supervisor said he had another job for me that better suited my talents. He led me to an area where another accommodation building was to be; there, a man was digging a hole with a pneumatic jackhammer. After introducing me to the civvy who had already dug one hole and was starting on the second, he left us. My new workmate showed me how to operate the compressor and pneumatic drill. We had to dig another three holes, each three feet deep and about twelve inches in diameter, to accommodate a twenty-foot wooden power pole. My associate asked if I had ever used a pneumatic drill before. When I replied in the negative, he said I looked as if I could do with some muscle building. I looked at his physique and understood his comment. He was probably 5' 6" high, when you looked at him; he was like a triangle, the point downwards. He had massive shoulders and arms complete with all the relevant muscle goes with that kind of build, not unlike the old style cartoon characters of my youth. Whereas me, I was reminiscent of a 6'2" beanpole! After demonstrating to me how to use the pneumatic drill, he invited me to try my hand. It looked so easy when he did it. As soon as I pulled the lever and the air pressure activated the drill, it promptly jumped out of my hands and the hole, dumping me on the ground. He obviously found the situation highly hilarious and had great difficulty controlling his laughter as he pulled me up onto my feet. I tried again, this time with a lot more success, my body vibrating in tune with the heavy equipment.

He stood watching me for 10 minutes or so and then said I should carry on whilst he nipped over to the office. I never saw him again until after lunch, he checked what I had done, saying that I seemed to have got the hang of it quickly. He stood by watching my efforts, then said he would be back shortly; and disappeared for the rest of the day.

Enjoying my newfound capabilities, I soldiered on during the rest of the afternoon, stopping in time to get myself cleaned up in the showers, before going on to the cookhouse for a meal. Walking into the shower block, I caught sight of myself in a mirror. Who was that ghostly figure looking back at me from under a thick coating of white dust? As I showered, a thick layer of white coral sludge quickly covered the floor. Then before I had finished my shower the water pressure dropped right off to nil, this situation would prevail throughout our stay at Maralinga. It was only if you were lucky did you get to fully shower, the rest just wiped off in the towel.

As I walked to the cookhouse, I realised that my whole body was still vibrating, and my hands were shaking. It was not until I sat down at the table to eat my meal that I really noticed the shaking. My mates thought it was highly hilarious when I tried to drink from my mug of tea and slopped up it all over the table. Getting food into my mouth was also a trial and error job. Even when I went to bed, my body still trembled and hands shook, by this time my back and arms were beginning to ache. A very restless night followed, not only as a result of the vibration from the pneumatic drill, but also that blasted Safari bed had a lot to answer for. Next morning at 08.00hrs, I returned to my hole digging to find my associate waiting by the machine. He took over digging for about 15 minutes and then said he was going over to the office and would see me later. I did some more digging for another half-hour and then switched the air compressor off. During the previous evening, I had realised that he had been taking me for a fool. Whilst I worked on, he was skiving off; I was doing the work whilst he was picking up the pay! Well, two can play at that game!

With the compressor shut down, I left the drill in the hole and wandered over to cookhouse for a cup of tea, then to the orderly room where I picked up an empty folder and put some blank paper in it. I was now equipped for my own skiving operation. For the next couple of days I wandered around the office complexes with my folder under my arm, having a look around. It was surprising how easy it was to enter into some of the laboratories there. No one bothered me, or questioned my presence there. Security? What security? Not that I was a likely threat to any one, I stopped for a cup of tea and a natter with some of the scientific people there; I was just a nosy parker. Maybe the two stripes on my arm gave me a certain air of authenticity.

Reg Simpson

One morning just as we were about to disperse to our temporary jobs, there was a change of plan; we were loaded onto transport and driven down to the airstrip. There was work to do in getting our dispersal area ready to receive the Canberras. At the airstrip, we split into two parties, one to work there, the other, my party out on to the airfield to set out the runway lighting, a necessary and useful facility, for any aircraft landing at night!

At lunchtime, that day, news came that our accommodation would be ready for us that evening. Thank god for that, no more 'Beds – Safari' and dusty concrete floors, why I thought that I do not know. There was no doubt, that the expectations for our new accommodation were high. Back from the airstrip that evening at the fire station, the same warrant officer as when we first arrived met us. Who again, I think almost gleefully, imparted the news that our new accommodation was ready; we would be living under canvas in two-man tents! He said that he was not to blame for this new accommodation, but that there simply was nothing else available. The building originally designated for us, had not yet been vacated by the civilian contractors who were running way behind on their construction schedule. We might not like the fact that we had to live under canvas, but that was all that was available. Was there to be no respite from the dreaded 'Beds – Safari'?

Reading from a list of names on his clipboard, he issued tent numbers to those names. To make things more enjoyable, there were not enough tents to accommodate us all, but not to worry; the warrant officer had a solution for that as well. For the dozen or so of us who had not had a tent number allocated, found ourselves allocated to a structure behind the Australian Air Force living quarters, that looked not unlike a wartime barrage balloon. It was in fact a dome shaped inflatable temporary warehouse about 40 feet long and 20 feet wide, inflatable ribs running from side to side held the structure up, whilst at the bottom an inflated rib running around the structure, was secured to the ground with ties and stakes at about 18 inch centres. Lugging our kit, bedding and Safari beds, we set out our bed spaces; at least we each had plenty of space.

Our new accommodation would be closer to the 'thunder-boxes', these were situated about 10 yards beyond our new home. This was more convenient than the more than one hundred yards that we had previously to traverse from the fire station each time you needed to answer a call of nature. The 'thunder-boxes' were unique to Maralinga and a version of field latrines that I had not seen before. The now empty, very large crate that had previously housed the fuselage and wings of a Swift aircraft made an excellent vehicle for conversion to housing for a latrine block. The aircraft itself was in the desert close to point Zero, as part of the plan to test the effects of the detonation on military equipment. The interior of the thunder boxes was rudimentary; there were six cubicles down one side, each separated by a hessian screen, leaving a walkway to the front. Each cubicle contained a chemical type toilet can with a lidded seat. The whole thing made no deference to privacy. Whilst the hessian screen separated you from your neighbour, they were wide open to the front.

There were a couple of drawbacks to the thunder boxes. Firstly, during most of the daylight hours they became nauseatingly stifling hot in the 120°+F temperatures, added to which were the mingled fumes of chemicals and human waste. Secondly, flies.
Due to the stench and the flies, there was a decided art to using this contraption during the day, requiring a bit of military precision.
a) Before using the cubicle, you peered in through the doorway to locate a vacant cubicle.
b) Back outside in the fresh air, you then took as deep a breath as possible and held it.
c) Dash inside to the cubicle, loosening your clothes as necessary.

d) Lift the lid and sit down smartly.
*(This last action needed to be swiftly coordinated, and was
essential to defeat the flies on two fronts.
Lifting the lid would give a chance for those flies inside the can, the
opportunity of getting outside. Sitting down smartly would deny the
squadrons of flies hovering above the can, the opportunity of
getting into the can.)*
e) Finally, try not to breathe whilst inside the thunder box. *(A feat
rarely achieved.)*
A slick exiting strategy was also called for.
Gather up your loins, stand-up and make a bolt for the doorway.
If you had found it necessary to take an extra breath or two whilst
sitting on the can, do not wait to throw up in the thunder box. Get
outside as quickly as possible into the fresh air, and deposit
whenever you had in your stomach onto the sand and kick more
sand over it, there was never any shortage of sand.
During the day, the more worldly wise of us forsook the niceties of
the thunder box by grabbing a shovel and wandering off into the
bush and doing your business. Even that had its own hazards, if you
were not careful where you squatted, you collected a backside full
of Spineafax spikes, which broke off and stayed there for many a
day. I was still getting some out of my ankles, and other places, two
years later.

That first evening in our new accommodation was more palatable
after a couple of hours in the 'wet' canteen. We were ready for bed
when we returned. Sleep did not come easily due to the
uncomfortable nature of the Safari bed.
During the early hours of the morning, my fitful night's slumber
was further disturbed, by shouting and cursing amongst my
colleagues; it was pitch black and I could see nothing. Carefully
trying to pull myself into a sitting position so as not to tip my bed
over (an inherent defect in the stupid beds), I came to a stop; I

could not get up. Something with a rubbery smell was covering my face. I flopped back on the bed, which promptly collapsed underneath me; I felt around with my hands and discovered the rubbery substance was covering me completely. Thinking I would suffocate, I panicked; then controlled myself and tried to think rationally. As my head had been against the bottom rib, I reasoned that I should be able to lift that rib up and slide myself under it to the outside; easier said than done! I managed to slide both hands under the rib and could feel cold night air outside, pushing with my feet I tried to push my body out; I could not! Panic set in again, I was panting for breath, as the covering seemed to cling to my face. I was sweating with all the effort; and the fear did not help either. I realised that the answer to sliding out underneath the rib was to remove one of the stakes. Moving my hands left and right I located a stake, with both hands on it I frantically tried to manoeuvre it; left and right, backwards and forwards, it did not appear to be moving. Suddenly it became loose in my hands, now I had room to slide my body to the outside. What a relief to be in the fresh cool air. I stood there for a few seconds recovering, before turning my attention to my colleagues, to see if they needed help. As I moved towards were the lad next to me was, I shivered violently. It was only then that I noticed that I was stark naked except for my wristwatch; as I slid out from under the rib I must have pulled my pyjama trousers off. What the hell, it did not matter, I was hundreds of miles out in the middle of the Aussie outback, and I wasn't suffocating anymore!

I helped the lad next to me out by the same route as I had taken; he wanted to know why I had no clothes on. Some of the others had made their escape via the doorway, a wooden structure still standing, albeit somewhat drunkenly. By the time everyone was outside the sun was coming up; it would soon be time for breakfast! In the light of the fast rising sun, we could see the once inflated warehouse was now a floppy, crumpled, partially inflated heap.

Reg Simpson

Word must have reached the warrant officer who arrived on the scene wanting to know what had happened. Standing next to me, he said, "Cpl. Simpson isn't it?"

"Yes Sir!"

It always concerned me when higher ranks with whom I had little contact knew my name. One of the tricks you soon learn in the services was to be as invisible as possible, to avoid being 'volunteered' for something.

"Why haven't you got any clothes on? You're going to give the dingoes and kangaroos around here a hell of a fright mate! What happened?"

"I don't know other than it looks as if the thing has collapsed."

He suddenly seemed all- knowledgeable about how we found ourselves in this predicament. "When we erected it this morning, it had a puncture, which we repaired. It was just before lunch when we inflated it. During the inflation period, it was at the hottest time of the day when the air would be hot and thin. I reckon the patch did not hold and was leaking, and then during the night as the outside air temperature dropped, the inflated air temperature cooled, the ribs just collapsed. Get these lads together, make sure you all get your gear from under that mess, and make your way back to the fire station, which is still empty. And I'll see you all after breakfast!"

Amidst a great deal of cursing, we fought our way under the mess that had been our home for the night, and rescued our bits and pieces. I remembered to get myself dressed before proceeding to the fire station. Once there, I put my bed back together and dumped my gear on it before heading to the showers.

The news of the incident had spread rapidly, as I found out in the cookhouse when I sat down at the table that I always shared with my mates. They found it highly hilarious to hear that I had been prancing around the bush in the dead of night, stark naked to boot!

Matters did not improve when I said, expecting sympathy, that I had thought I was going to suffocate under that rubbery substance. Someone made the suggestion that whoever had tried to put the patch on, should be given a medal for trying to put me out of this world.

Back at the fire station, we hung around until the warrant officer showed up. When he did, he imparted the good news that by lunchtime he would have some more two-man tents erected which we could use. That was something I was not looking forward to; I had been hoping for something a little more civilised.
When I eventually arrived down at the airstrip, it seemed that everyone there knew about the night's adventures. I came in for a great deal of ribbing.

At lunchtime, the warrant officer was waiting for us at the fire station, to issue us with our tent numbers; mine was G 2. I decided to identify where the tent was located on my way to the cookhouse for lunch; then after lunch, I would move my gear.
Whilst humping my kit etc. on the way to the tents I heard someone calling my name; it was Mick Foran, the Corporal in charge of the admin office. He had heard about our little problem overnight and had a solution for me. He had found himself a two-bedded room next to the Aussie accommodation. He offered for me to share with him if I wanted. We went to look at his room; it was about 10ft x 10ft, one of six in a single storey wood framed building clad in corrugated iron. It was basic, but far superior to living in a tent on a Safari bed; this had a proper iron framed bed with a real mattress, a steel single wardrobe and a very small wooden bedside cabinet. I readily accepted his offer, dropped my kit on the spare bed; it was with great relish that I took my hated Safari bed to tent G2 which was still unoccupied, and tossed it inside, and good riddance! My

new home was only twenty yards from the cookhouse and close to the showers; life was looking up!

We had been at Maralinga for about two weeks, when the welcome news came that our aircraft were coming up from Edinburgh field. The next morning it was back to normal RAF life as the Canberras arrived. Over the next three weeks, life was relaxed with the aircraft making usually two flights a day as the crews flew familiarisation flights in the area and practiced the manoeuvres they would make when collecting cloud samples. As an Armourer, there was little work to occupy my time; no bomb gear to work on, just the ejection seats to maintain. My work was limited to pre-flight and after flight inspections. Consequently, I was often a 'go-fer' for our Flight Sergeant, one of my many 'go-fer' duties was to ferry special packages that arrived on incoming aircraft, from the airstrip up to the Village up on the hill. That's how I came to meet Bill Penny; most of my packages were for him. We also assisted with the unloading of cargo for the scientific people; the many crates to an inquiring mind, containing mystery items. On one particular occasion, I had to supervise a detail of six men to unload cargo from two Hastings aircraft onto two flatbed trucks; the crates contained sheep and goats.

Waiting to collect them from me was one of the scientific people I had met whilst 'touring' the office complex. I frivolously asked if he was starting a farm; if so, being a country boy I knew how to milk animals and was willing to help. He said he was not going to start farming. When pressed as to their use in the middle of a desert, he replied that they were for use during the tests to measure blast and heat effects, but I should not tell anyone he had said so,. Unfortunately, some of my detail overheard his remarks. There was some dissent from three of them regarding the ethics of what they just heard and they did not want to carry on the unloading and therefore become involved. I had to remind them that we were in no position to question anything regarding the tests. Orders are orders, or face the music. The three of them in question were townies and had no real animal contact of this nature before, whereas, I as a country boy probably had a closer relationship with the animals than they did. The most vociferous of them was close to tears as we continued the offloading. I must admit that I felt quite guilty myself as we unloaded them, knowing what their fate would be, terrible burns and disfigurement, at the best, a quick and painless death.

In early September prior to the start of the weapon tests - there would not be time once they had started - there was a local international agreement with our Aussie drinking buddies in the 'wet' canteen, that we should have our own mini international test match, Poms v. Aussies for the Maralinga Ashes. The Aussies were always looking for an opportunity to put one over on the Poms; this might just be their chance.

Our two teams met on a Sunday if I remember correctly, the venue was somewhere out behind the fire station, on a dirt pitch the Aussies had constructed. A grass pitch would have been somewhat of a luxury, grass as we Poms recognised it, was very noticeable by its absence in the desert. As it transpired, it was their day, we Poms were utterly and totally thrashed. Our excuse was, that as English gentlemen, we only played on grass wickets, not sun baked, concrete hard, dirt. This kind of pitch gave our 'down-under cousins' a distinct advantage. Some of our team also took the not uncharitable view that their top fast bowler, an Aussie army man, was in fact a trained assassin, assigned the duty of killing, maiming or at the very least diminishing the 'Pommie' side to a quivering mass of jelly. If that is true, it is a miracle that he did not achieve his first two assignments, but he most certainly fulfilled the third.

Reg Simpson

We lost the toss and they chose to put us in to bat first. The opening pair was out so fast that the game had to wait, whilst the next of us got padded up. None of the first three had hit the ball, all being victims of the Aussie assassin. I was number four in the batting order, the others were out, without even hitting the ball; the man was fearsome. I faced up to him, determined that he was not going to get me out on the first ball, he did not, and I did not see the ball either, after it left his hand, all I heard was the 'thwack', as it slapped into the wicketkeeper's gloves. Having survived his first ball I was a little more confident now. I nervously faced up to his second ball, watching him as he took his long high-speed run up to the wicket, his arm rising up with the ball in it. I kept my eye on the ball as it flew towards me without bouncing, swinging wildly at it, truly believing that I was going to get 'six' off this ball. There was a stinging, tingling sensation in my hands as the ball hit the bat, rather than me hitting the ball. It hit the bat with such a tremendous force it ripped it from my grasp onto the stumps and back to the wicketkeeper. That was the end of any possible international test cricket career on my part! We had now lost three wickets for no runs in the first over; fortunately, they changed their bowler, it gave the rest of our team a chance. I believe that eventually our side, made the grand total of 45 runs, all out. Fortunately, I cannot recall how many runs the Aussies scored, I'm not sure anyone counted. It had been an ignominious defeat. For defeat, maybe you should read thrashing! The result was not unlike the ignominious results of the 2013 Ashes series in Australia.

It was with some considerable measure of relief after the cricket debacle, to get back to normal. We had pre-flighted our three aircraft for what I thought was another sortie of practice runs. I was helping our Flight Commander to strap himself into his ejection seat when he said to me, "Well, get in! You're coming with us!" I could hardly believe my luck. I had been pestering him with my requests for a flight, to no avail for the last few days; now unexpectedly, my luck had changed.

When I said I should get a parachute from the safety equipment section, expecting that I would have to ride on the fold down seat just inside the door, he said I should not bother. On take-off and landing, I could use the Bomb aimer's ejection seat. He reminded me that I had I had told him several times that if I ever had the chance, I would not hesitate to use an ejection seat, as I trusted them implicitly. I had previously told him about my Martin Baker works detachment; and how I had ridden the test rig seat three times.

Once we were airborne, he said I should go forward into the Bomb aimer's bombing position, and lie in there looking forward and down at the ground. It was with great excitement that I strapped myself into the ejection seat. I knew that several of my colleagues watching as we taxied out to the runway, would be extremely envious. Several of us had requested a flight, only to be given a definite 'no'. Now, here I was, about to go airborne to the envy of many.

We roared down the runway and lifted off. Over the headset, the pilot said I should come forward. I unstrapped myself, laying the straps out so that I could quickly get back into them should the need arise. I lay down, looking out through the plexiglass at the vast expanse of the Australian bush. All I could see was red sand and bush, which stretched as far as the eye could see. The pilot gave me a running commentary of where we were, and flew over the actual ground zero points for the forthcoming tests. We flew slowly over them watching the men working below. Then the pilot spoke to the other two pilots and they appeared one either side of us, and slightly below. My pilot said I should hold tight, I heard the engines gain power, and as we gained speed the ground passing below was a blur. I heard him say, "Corporal, Maralinga airstrip is five miles ahead on your right. We will fly past in formation at 500 feet." I saw the air strip and buildings flash past. There was more talk between the pilots and we were turning.

My pilot spoke again, "Corporal, we're going to do another flypast, this time at 200 feet and as we pass the flight line we are going to do a Prince of Wales feathers break. So hold on tight, we will go vertical and our wingmen will go left and right in a shallow climb. I looked for something to hold on to, and found the base of the framework of the bombsight, gripping it tightly in my left hand and my right gripping a frame on the right side of the cockpit. I laid there looking down onto the bush and sand, we were diving at a shallow angle, the ground flashing by. I looked to my right and saw the buildings at the flight line come into view. Over my headset, I heard our pilot call "Break!" The ground disappeared from view, immediately replaced by blue sky. My body was sliding back down the padding I was laying on. I was sliding seemingly ever backwards I gripped even tighter to the bombsight framework. I hung on for grim life! My stomach was being dragged ever downwards and felt as though it was going to end up in my boots. I had never felt the effects of gravity so severely before. As the G-forces reduced I realized that we had levelled out and I relaxed. Upon instructions from the pilot, I strapped myself back into the ejection seat. The other two aircraft were on their approach for landing. We took our turn in making our approach for landing, as we taxied back to the flight line the navigator who I was sat next to, gave me the thumbs up sign, grinning, he asked how I felt. "Great!" I lied, with what I thought was a grin. It was more likely to have been a grimace. I was still trying to re-orientate my senses. With the aircraft parked and engines shut down, I clambered out onto the concrete. The pilot followed me, as we stood on the concrete; he asked if I had enjoyed the flight. I confirmed I had, but was not sure if my stomach was still with me. He said, at least I had not spewed my guts up, due to the violent climb and dive back down to make our landing approach. They had thought that I might. He did not know how close I had been to having to clean the cockpit of vomit, very close! It was tradition that if anyone in the cockpit 'threw up', they had to clean it all up. A not very pleasant job, because you had to get rid of the smell as well. The floor of the cockpit had all manner of crooks and crannies to get into, very difficult to clean!.

The Flight Commander, said that they had decided to take me on this flight as a 'thank you' for ensuring their ejection seats were always ready for use. I was appreciative of their gesture and said so.
It was not until I was discussing my flight with a couple of my envious friends, that I realized that the date was 15th September. It was the Battle of Britain anniversary day. How could I have been so ignorant? On the other hand, life was so far from normal, one tended to lose track of the days.

Reg Simpson

Chapter 7: The Great Sound & Light Spectaculars.

Film badges were issued to all the ground crew a few days prior to the first test on 27th September. These were supposed to indicate if we ha d been exposed to any radioactivity. It did not measure the amount, only the volume of exposure indicated by the level of darkness of the film when developed. In the days before the test during a briefing, we learnt that when the aircraft returned from their mission in the cloud they would be radioactively 'hot', and that we would have to wear protective clothing to carry out any work on them. The protective clothing comprised a one piece white cotton coverall complete with drawstring hood and elasticated sleeve and ankle cuffs, white cotton gloves to be tucked in under the elasticated cuffs, Wellington boots with the elasticated trouser leg cuffs pulled down over the top of the Wellingtons and lastly, a simple nose and mouth mask. The mask was very similar to the simple dust mask of today. The procedure on arrival for work was thus; we would enter the decontam building from the clean side, remove all our everyday clothing including underclothes and hang them on a peg on the wall. Donning the above protective clothing, we could then proceed to work on the aircraft. After the work was completed, we would re-enter the decontam building from the 'dirty' side, be cleansed and declared safe. Only then could we step into the 'clean' area and get dressed, before stepping back out into the real world.

One of our main entertainment sources in the evenings was the radio, television was in its' infancy and not in general usage those days. One of the highlights was the episodes of the 'Goon Show', much appreciated if you had that kind of humour. One particular joke we found very relevant to our situation was when,

Reg Simpson

Harry Seccombe said, 'Owing to a strike at the Air Ministry, there will be no weather tomorrow'. This was highly appropriate as we had just been advised on site that the first detonation was delayed due to unsuitable weather for the following day.

On the day of the first test code named 'One Tree' on 27th of September, we dispatched the designated aircraft on their mission. Those of us, who would not be involved in recovering the samples from the returning aircraft, were offered the chance to go up to the forward area, about 20 miles north of the airstrip and witness the detonation right of the weapon from that vantage point, approximately 3 miles (?) distant. After an undulating ride, (we were riding across an ancient seabed) in an old RAAF wooden slatted seat bus, we arrived at the forward area. Dominating the centre was a large concrete structure, a safe place for the scientists to be, when the blast occurred. We joined the quite large group of people that already had assembled there; looking around there was a large variety of people. There were many military officers from other countries together with our own Navy, Army and Air Force. A great number of media and newsreel people with lots of cameras set on tripods. It was as usual a beautiful sunny day, clear blue sky and not a cloud in sight. The sun was its usual scorching hot at this time of day, my tunic top was stoking wet with perspiration, so I took it off and did a bit of 'vertical' sunbathing. Thank goodness, we did not have to wear our protective clothing.

At five minute intervals the loudspeakers barked out a message, **i.e." Zero minus 40 minutes."**
About 30 minutes before zero time, the loudspeakers barked into life with a message advising us of the countdown procedure prior to the detonation.
At Minus 5 minutes, we should all turn facing south and stay that way.

The countdown would continue at one-minute intervals.
At Minus1 minute, we should close our eyes; place the palms of our hands over our eyes. The countdown would continue at one-second intervals until zero.
When we are aware of a brilliant flash, we could remove our hands; open our eyes, and turnaround to face north again.
The countdown continued on its relentless downward trend.
"Zero Minus 5 Minutes. Everyone turn to the south."
Several marshals ensured that we were all facing south.
The count continued downwards.
"Zero minus 1 Minute. Close your eyes. Put your hands over your eyes and keep eyes shut until you see the flash."
"Zero minus 30 seconds."
It seemed a long time waiting for zero, whoever was doing the countdown was totally devoid of excitement. His voice was consistently deadpan.
"Zero minus 5 Seconds!"
"Zero minus 4 Seconds"
"Zero minus 3 Seconds"
"Zero minus 2 Second!"
"Zero minus 1 Second!"
"ZERO!"

As the sound of 'Zero' died away, there was an intense ultra-brilliant white flash of light. With my eyes tightly closed behind my hands, I could see all the bones in my hands just as if in an x-ray and I could see all the people who were standing around me. I dropped my hands, opened my eyes and turned round to the North as instructed, to see a most beautiful sight as the gigantic fireball rose up from the ground. Almost at the same instant, a terrific heat flash swept over us, probably no more than two seconds and it was gone. It was so hot, that after it had gone I shivered for a moment in spite of the terrific Aussie daytime heat. It was not unlike walking past the open door of a big furnace. A second or two later there was a dull double boom in the distance. I turned to my colleague next to me and said that I thought that it had been a bit of an anti-climax.

Hardly had the words left my mouth when, there was an enormous 'bang'; like nothing I had ever heard before, it hurt my ear drums and vibrated through my head, and left me with a ringing noise in my ears for several minutes after. Within seconds, the shock wave hit us. It was so violent that I staggered, the ground vibrated violently under me; resonating within and shaking my body. To my left I saw one of the newsreel camera-tripods fall over and the operator trying to grab it. As the ground vibrated, little dust devils about 6 inches high emanated from the dusty sand we stood on. The shockwave effect on my body, was so severe that it felt that the whole of the inside of my body was vibrating, making me feel unstable and nauseous. The violent machinations of my whole being, felt as if I was going to fall to pieces.

I was in awe and exhilarated at what I had just witnessed. I had seen some spectacular sights on my Bomb Disposal duties; this however was something far superior, way beyond my expectations. The multi-coloured fireball with its vivid yellows, oranges and reds was enormous; as it slowly rose into the sky, it appeared to be boiling furiously within itself. As the seconds and minutes ticked by the boiling fireball continued rising and rising into clear blue sky, as it did so, it formed a boiling mushroom shaped cloud supported on a slender rising column of smoke and debris. This truly massively awesome sight for me as an Armourer was almost indescribable, in short – bloody fantastic! It was incredible that I was able to be this close to it. My RAF life revolved around detonating explosives, but that as the Americans say, was 'chicken shit' by comparison. With this weapon, Great Britain could once again hold its head up and be amongst the world's leading nations;

a country that should not be underestimated; even if our politicians were a bunch of self-serving, wailing nincompoops.

I never gave a passing thought as to the likelihood of any possible danger to my colleagues or myself. I trusted implicitly that Bill Penny, his staff and my military superiors would safeguard my welfare. The future years might tell me if my implicit trust was misplaced or not. It was almost impossible to take my eyes off that spectacularly impressive sight.

Our ogling time was up and we had to return to the airstrip. With one lingering last look at the cloud, which was very high in the sky and beginning to bend over at the top as the high-level winds took hold of it, I climbed aboard the bus for the journey south, back to the airstrip. On the journey, there was much animated discussion of what we had seen. I think that like me some of the lads were highly impressed with what we had witnessed. After 10 minutes or so, all conversation ceased and no doubt, we were all deep in our own thoughts.

Back at the airstrip, one of the cloud-sampling Canberras was taxying onto the restricted parking area and came to a stop as we de-bussed. I watched as two of our ground crew who had not been at the forward area met the aircraft. Both were dressed in white one-piece hooded protective type suits, cotton gloves, and a simple dust filter mask over their nose and mouth. Whilst one taped a protective tube onto the crew access door, to enable the pilot and navigator to cleanly exit the aircraft without contaminating their flying suits. The other was at one of the wingtip pods and using a long pair of special tongs pulled what I assumed was the filter from the pod and placed it into a container that was on the ground. I did not get a chance to see anything else, as we had to go and change into protective gear ourselves.

Reg Simpson

Later that afternoon one of the pilots took the official photo of the test for issue to the newspapers down to RAAF Edinburgh Field for distribution. As I was helping him strap himself into the ejection seat, he let me have a quick look at it. Disappointing really, it was black and white and nothing like the glorious colour version, I had seen earlier. The cloud sampling continued over the next few days, enabling us to get more familiar with working in our protective gear, and the continual monitoring by the safety people.

The morning after this first test, having missed the transport, I was walking with another colleague down to the airstrip. We had reached roughly the halfway point between the village and the airstrip when car pulled up alongside us. The back window wound down, a figure from inside said, "Can I give you lads a lift?"
We gratefully clambered in, and I saw it was Bill Penny who recognised me.
"Well, Cpl. Simpson, what did you think of our little exercise yesterday?"
I said that I thought that was simply fantastic and went on to recall my impressions of the previous day. I did wonder if I might have gone over the top a bit in my excitement about the explosion because he was laughing and said, "If only everyone, the CND for example, was as enthusiastic about it as you are!"
He went on to say, that nuclear weapons were a new science and technology and no one knew all the answers yet. Knowing that we would be working on the cloud sampling aircraft, he said we should closely follow all the safety precautions that were in place, they were designed for our safety. By this time, we were down at the airstrip; he dropped us off and drove away to the forward area.
My colleague was quite impressed with my 'socialising with the bigwigs' as he put it, and wanting to know how Bill Penney knew me. I explained my part-time job as a 'go-fer'.

A few days after the test, whilst at the airstrip the chance came to visit the forward area again, this time to view the crater resulting from the explosion. We climbed aboard the bone shaking bus and made our way to the forward area. As we drove towards point zero I noticed that scattered around the area were various military vehicles, artillery pieces, a Swift aircraft and other equipment badly damaged and in various stages of destruction. The guide told us that all the equipment we saw, was specifically placed to assess the destructive force of the weapon .We drove slowly past the crater at a distance of probably 50 yards; we could not get off the bus. By standing up on the bus to give us better elevation we could see into the crater. All that I remember of it is, seeing a very large crater the sides of which appeared to have a green-blue glass covering. According to our guide, the tremendous heat of the explosion melted the sand into a glass like compound. It was all a world of wonderment, and I found it all extremely interesting, not only from an armament point of view.

Two more tests took place, one on 4th October (Marcoo) and another on 11th October (Kite). The sites for these tests were approximately 20 miles distant. When these detonations took place we were restricted to the flight area and dressed in protective gear. At zero hour we still had to turn to the south, and follow the procedures as we had done when up at the forward area. Whilst the light flash was less intense than the first one, it was still possible to see the bones in your hands. There was no heat flash; ground vibration was much less violent.

The test on 11th of October code-named 'Kite' was very significant; it was the first airdrop by a British aircraft of a viable nuclear weapon. The Valiant aircraft that was to make the drop had been parked outside of a 'secure' building about four hundred yards to the West of our flight line for several days. Despite strict instructions to keep away from the area, a couple of us had decided to go up there and have a look to see if we could see the bomb. It proved to be a fruitless exercise; as soon as we got within about 100 yards of the building, heavily armed Australian Army Police appeared from no-where and intercepted us. They warned us off in no uncertain terms, and language.

How did the bomb get there? Did it arrive on the Valiant in an unarmed state, or, did they build it there at Maralinga? I don't know and probably never will! Security there was better than that in the laboratories! Maybe there was nothing in the labs to be secure about; who knows?

The final test on 22nd October took place in darkness just before midnight. As a spectacle, this was different from the others. After the usual roll call to account for everyone, dressed in all our protective clothing we paraded on our restricted area hard standing, as by now all our aircraft were radioactively hot and had to be parked in a special 'contaminated area', where we would be shortly commencing the decontamination of the three aircraft. We prepared for zero hour as in all other tests by turning to face south with eyes closed and hands over our eyes (in this case cotton gloved hands) and waited.

At zero hour, there was a vividly intense brilliant white flash of light, increased in its intensity due to the darkness, which surrounded us. This was quite unlike any of the other light flashes, because of its intensity. Not only could I as usual, see all the bones in my hands, but also I could see all my colleagues dressed in white, could see their faces in detail and recognise them. Not only that, but the light reflected off of the various aircraft types parked in front of the terminal building, to the extent that I could recognise the type and read their identification numbers and see all the rivets in the aircraft skin. It was as if the detail was broad daylight, yet the light appeared to be silvery. It was unnerving. Dropping my hands and opening my eyes, I turned to the North. I could see nothing new, only what I had been seeing through my hands previously. It was as though those reflections had burned into my optical system and brain, the detail was incredible and very vivid. It took a couple of minutes or so or my eyes to revert back to normal, by which time – yes I had heard the bang, and yes I had felt the ground tremble, but it was of no significance compared to the visual effect of the light flash. I realised I had not been seeing things when my colleagues started reporting and comparing similar visions. It was the main topic of conversation for the rest of the shift.

Next morning at the airstrip, someone, from the radiological department collected my film badge from me. It was the first and only film badge issued to me. The previous night's visions continued to be the topic of the day. Until that was, an Australian National Airlines aircraft touched down on the runway, and finally parked in front of the terminal building. Two attractive Airhostesses came down the steps. All reminiscences of the previous night's visions ceased, as we watched the spectacle unfolding in front of us, the Airhostesses made their way from the plane into the terminal building.

Could we be seeing more light flash visions? No, this was something more realistic, two live women. The first we had seen after nearly 3 months in the desert. So it was true after all, women did exist in the world! Oh boy! Oh boy!

An hour or so later, a group of passengers, (scientists and media people), were ushered onto the aircraft by those visions of loveliness, and the aircraft departed.

We had to put that latest vision into the backs of our minds, and turn our attention to the job for which we were there.

Reg Simpson

Chapter 8: Who's for an Irradiated Shower?

There were several sampling sorties over the next three days and the aircraft needed servicing. Finally, the sampling sorties were over. With the aircraft parked on the decontamination hard standing, a new and interesting phase of this assignment was about to commence, a phase which could have life-threatening consequences for us all. The day before radiological decontamination of the Canberras commenced, those of us detailed to be part of the team, gathered at the decontamination building for a briefing. Wing Commander Urquhart who had overall responsibility for aircraft decontamination, carried out the briefing. He introduced another RAF officer, with the rank of Flying Officer, who would be the officer in charge of us. I do not remember the surname of this officer, but to this day, I still refer to him as 'Martin', I believe it was his first name, more about that later.

I have always remembered the Wingco's first words. **"The work which you are about to undertake for the next few days or so, is extremely dangerous. Make no mistake; exposure to uncontrolled high levels of radiation can kill you. Follow the rules and you will be safe.**

I don't know about my colleagues, but I took his words to heart. It reminded me of my first day on bomb disposal when our Bomb Disposal Officer said to me, "When we detonate this bomb, keep your head down below ground level in the dugout. If you don't, whilst the shrapnel may miss you, the blast will rip your face apart. I don't want to have to write a letter to your mother, telling her what a prat you had been by not following orders."
Some things stick vividly in the mind!
The Wingco went on to tell us, we would be working on the highly radioactive surfaces of the aircraft. They (sic), had to reduce their

high radiation levels to a much lower acceptable safe level whereby making them safe for every day working. The planned method of achieving this would be by steam cleaning the exterior skin of the aircraft; copious washing and scrubbing with a long handled broom and high-pressure water hoses. However, if we followed the instructions of the decontamination monitors, regarding the safety procedures that we should follow implicitly; we would be safe. Before handing us over to the decontamination supervisor, he had one last piece of information for us. Due to the extreme heat during the day, we would be operating from 04.00hrs until 11.00hrs when the ambient temperatures started to became too high for us to work. Breakfast would be at 03.30hrs!

The decontamination supervisor took over the briefing. He detailed the protective wear that we would be using. A one piece white cotton coverall complete with drawstring hood and elasticated sleeve and ankle cuffs, white cotton gloves to be tucked in under the elasticated cuffs, Wellington boots with the elasticated trouser leg cuffs pulled down over the top of the Wellingtons and lastly, a simple thin nose and mouth mask. The mask was very similar to the simple everyday dust mask of today – 'not much use to man nor beast'! (My words – not his.)
The procedure on arrival for work was thus; we would enter the decontam building from the clean side, remove all our everyday clothing including underclothes and hang them on a peg on the wall. We would don a clean dry coverall, gloves, wellingtons and mask, ready to take on the might of radiation!
There then followed a listing of the pertinent rules on how the system would operate.
1. It was highly important not to breach the segregation of clean and dirty areas of the decontamination building at all times.
2. It was imperative that we wore our full protective clothing at all times when on the 'dirty' side of the area.

3. There would be a meal break at approximately 07:00 hours and at which time we would have to go through the decontamination procedure from dirty to clean. Before returning to work, we would put on clean protective gear before going back into the dirty area. Very importantly**, no food or drink whilst you are 'dirty'.**
4. If for any reason you needed to leave the dirty work area, you must enter the decontamination building from the 'dirty' side, and go through the decontamination procedure.

What is very pertinent to note at this stage is, that there was at no time, any mention of the subject of film badges or dosimeters. How would they know how to what level of radiation to which we had been exposed to? There was no mention of how anyone was going to monitor or measure such levels. Whilst the tests were taking place, I always had a film badge secured to the waistband of my trousers. When the tests were complete, and before we started any 'decontam' operations, my film badge, together with those of my colleagues were collected from us, which was the last we saw of them or their like. I recall at the time wondering why the 'decontam' man always wore a measuring device and we did not.

In my naivety, I guess my trust was in my superiors to look after me, especially as in the essence of the Wingco's words, 'the work that you are doing is extremely dangerous and could kill you if you don't follow the set procedures'. My job as an Armourer was working with explosives and I think that they carried the same kind of tag line, so those words were part of my daily life in any case.

The words 'You will be safe,' were different, they were somehow comforting. Why should I not trust my superiors, it was their responsibility?

There is also another aspect, I had been in the services long enough to know, orders are orders; it was not my prerogative to

Reg Simpson

question such orders. You cannot have the scenario where junior ranks challenge the decisions of their superior ranks; that is what discipline is all about.

Inside the decontamination building, was a large area, probably 20' x 20' divided into two sections by what looked like to wooden PT benches from school days. One side of which was the 'clean' side, with the entry door from the rest of the world. The other side, about twice the size of the clean side was the 'dirty' area, with a door leading to our work area.
When we were ready and properly dressed to start work, we simply stepped over the bench from the clean side, into the dirty area and exited the door to the work area. Simple!

What was not so simple, was the procedure followed when coming back into in the dirty area from the work area. Firstly, you took off your boots and put them in a designated area then gloves and coverall into specially marked bins. Then you gave yourself a good wash down with soap and water in the hot showers. When you had finished, the 'decontam' man ran a Geiger counter all over your body including the soles of your feet, and if you were still 'hot', you went back into the showers again. It was quite a common occurrence to have to repeat showering up to four times before the monitor gave you the OK. There was one occasion when I had to have five showers; heaven only knows what was sticking to my head. After you had dried yourself, you then went to a machine where you stood on a metal plate and put your hands into two slots on the machine front. If the alarm sounded, you had to go back through the showering process repeatedly until such times, as you were acceptable. For a bit of fun, and to annoy the 'decontam' man, when you were stood on this machine, if you grabbed hold of something that was 'dirty', and then shoved your hand into one of the slots, this immediately set off the alarm. This was very much to the consternation of the decontamination man, and taboo to boot. The decontam man always had the last laugh, he made you go for another shower(s) until he determined you were clean. Once you had the 'all clear' from that machine, you could enter the clean area, get dressed, and leave the building.

I had not given much thought to getting up at 03:00hrs to shave and shower, be at the cookhouse for breakfast at 03:30 hours and then onto the rickety old bus them to the airstrip for 04:00hrs. We abandoned the shave and shower routine in the mornings after the first morning. We were going to be soaked to the skin for the entirety of our shift in any case. The first morning was a bit of a shock. Whilst the daytime temperatures soared to 120° +F, the early hours of the morning were a different matter; there was often frost on everything. It was not a suitable time of day to be about in tropical kit, i.e. shorts and a thin shirt. There was no question of us not being awake long before we got to the airstrip!
The Wingco and 'Martin' arrived just after us, they were not too happy about not having suitable clothing for these early-morning temperatures. The upshot was the issue of white submariners jerseys that afternoon; where they managed to find that kind of clothing in such short space of time I do not know. On second thoughts, there was a contingent of Australian Navy personnel on site so perhaps they were holding stocks. They must have been somewhat precious to someone, as we were each required to sign for our Jersey. When I signed for mine, I noticed that the price allocated to the item was £20 Australian, a fair bit of money in those days! We had to hand them back into the stores when we had completed the decontam work.

I was detailed to be in charge of one of the two crews of six other ranks. It was noticeable that there were no Senior NCOs in the cleaning teams, just corporals and below! In army terms - cannon

fodder. The cleaning of the aircraft was a simple and frequently frustrating exercise. With the aircraft parked on the special 'decontam' area, the first part of the operation was to thoroughly hose it down, then go all over it with a steam cleaner and brushes, then hose it down again. At this point, the 'decontam' man would run his Geiger- counter over the parts of the plane that he could reach from the ground, and pronounce his decision.
"Sorry, still too hot; you will have to do it again!"
It was a phrase we would hear over, and over, and over again, throughout our time whilst working on 'decontam'.

We worked from pairs of steps to gain access the top of the aircraft, moving about on the top of the aircraft was fraught with danger. Walking along the tops of the wings in Wellington boots, and masses of water made for a slippery job. However, the ultimate test of ability was balancing yourself as you walked along the top of the wet fuselage to get to the tail plane; acrobatic skills were a decided plus, when engaging in this manoeuvre. Looking back on that time as one who suffers with vertigo, I wonder whatever possessed me to get up there at all. Was I perhaps showing off my leadership skills? These days I think the answer is 'idiocy'. It was fortunate in that no one fell off, and was injured. The one occasion when I nearly became a statistic remains in my memory. I still remember that moment of panic when I recall it. I was lucky that I was able to avoid the situation by one of my more acrobatic moments; I slipped, and I am sure my heart skipped several beats as I mentally prepared myself for the pain that was to follow when I hit the ground. Somehow, I managed to regain my dignity and sit down astride the fuselage. Fortunately, the raucous laughter from my less than sympathetic colleagues helped me hide my fear. After that incident, it seemed that I was the only one ever doing the walking of the fuselage; when that was necessary the other members of my crew always seemed to be busily engaged in other activities. In

those days, health and safety was just common sense.
Whilst we were washing, scrubbing, and hosing down the aircraft, we were ourselves continually soaked to the skin with irradiated water. With the continual spray of water and the drenching you received when working under the wings there was no way of escaping it. The protective clothing was of no use whatsoever in protecting us from the irradiated water, as it went straight through the coveralls onto the body and collected in the Wellington boots.

On day two of the decontamination operation, the Wingco and Martin appeared on the scene at 07:00 hours. On the third day, the Wingco was on site as usual at 07:00 hours, but there was no sign of 'Martin'. He asked me if I had seen Flying Officer '...?...' I confirmed that I had not. From his comments about some Junior Officers, and what he might do when he found one, it was obvious that he was not happy. Telling me that he was going up to the Village to find him, he strode out of the 'clean area'. Just as I was walking back to the aircraft to start work again the Wingco returned, accompanied by 'Martin'.

Shortly after, Martin dressed in his protective gear approached me and said he was in deep mire with the 'Wingco'. I did not sympathise with him because in those days, one had to tread carefully around officers, who generally, did not want anything to do with the mere mortals of the lower ranks. He asked if I would help him every morning from now on, to ensure that he was on site before the Wingco arrived in the mornings. I agreed that I would. We were after all teammates, and he was the man in direct charge of us and never caused us any grief, although we rarely saw him on the job. He may have been an officer, but he was part of our team and in true RAF spirit, we always looked after one another. The plan was that at 06:00 hours I would take our transport and go up to the Junior Officers rooms and make sure he was awake, dressed and get him back to the decontamination block before the Wingco arrived on site at 07:00 hours. The plan was simple; the execution of it though was a very different matter. He advised me that he was likely to have many very 'heavy nights' in the officer's mess bar, making it very difficult for him to wake up in time to be on duty. He said that when attempting to wake him up in the mornings I should not 'faff' around with calling him 'Sir', because it probably wouldn't register, so therefore I should call in by his name, 'Martin'. To cut a long story short, every morning thereafter, I always, but sometimes with great difficulty, achieved in getting him down to the site and filled with black coffee prior to the arrival of the Wingco. When I say 'with great difficulty', I mean with great difficulty; most mornings I would have to physically force the door open, because he was asleep on the floor just inside the doorway where he had collapsed after shutting the door. In addition, I would have to fight the fumes of whisky and brandy, made more difficult with my aversion to both of these spirits. It was the side of the 'officer class' that we normally did not see, it just goes to prove that the only difference between them and us, is a probable higher education and a Queens Commission!

My early morning activities were not as I thought, known only to 'Martin' and myself. A couple of our aircrew jokingly - I think - asked if my 'batman' services were available to other officers, such as themselves. Just before the 'decontam' activities ended, W/C Urquhart had been talking to my crew about our work. As he was leaving, he turned to me and said, "Corporal, thank you for your help in the early mornings." He nodded to me and grinned as he got in his vehicle. I really thought my 'batman' duties were a secret! It appears to have been an open secret in the Officer's mess.!

Aside from these extraneous duties, my team and I carried on the repetitive hosing down, steam cleaning, and hosing down again of the aircraft until it was declared to be at a safe level. This took several days of repetitive work. I lost count of the number of times we repeatedly washed the aircraft; it was just an ongoing repetitious exercise.

Whilst all this was ongoing, I recall that I was walking the perilous walk along the top of the fuselage of one of the Canberras, when we heard over the radio that Canberra bombers from Cyprus were bombing the Egyptian bases in the Suez Canal zone. The Suez crisis had commenced, and here was I in the middle of the vast Aussie outback washing down Canberras fitted with a 'gas bag' in the bomb bay instead of bombs. How I envied those armourers in Cyprus loading bombs into their bomb bays. We soon forgot the Suez crisis, there was more washing down of aircraft to be done.

Those aircraft must have seen more tons of water over them in that short space of time in the hot dry Aussie desert than they had ever seen in their whole lives. We the 'decontam' crew, on a rough ' back of the envelope calculation', must have spent a cumulative total period of at least 60 hours immersed in radioactive water, due to our continual drenching.

With the weapons tests, cloud sampling and 'decontam' completed, the Canberras returned to RAAF Edinburgh. We the ground crew, followed a few days later after loading all the ground equipment onto transport and tidying up the dispersal area. Some of the ground equipment was found to be contaminated with radioactivity, and had to have a 'wash and brush up' with the steam hose etc. before we could load it on to the transporting aircraft.

For some of our team the journey was not over. They would be transiting on, to Christmas Island in the Pacific Ocean, for participation in 'Operation Grapple'. This was Great Britain's trials of their first hydrogen bombs, which if successful would make us a fully-fledged nuclear nation with awesome firepower.

Reg Simpson

For me, the exciting times over, I found myself transferred to Operation Grapple 'X' Support Base at RAAF Edinburgh Field, South Australia. There, I was destined to be in charge of the Armament Section, life there was by comparison with Maralinga, dull and boring and so it remained until July 1957 when I returned to the UK.

The flight home was another bright episode on two counts. Firstly, the aircraft was a Comet 2C, an iconic world leading aircraft of its time. Secondly, the journey home from Australia to UK, via Singapore, Ceylon, Bahrain, El Adam (Libya) and finally RAF Lyneham Wiltshire, completed a round the world trip, courtesy of the UK government. In addition, there would be 14 days disembarkation leave.

My 14 days disembarkation leave turned into 34 days due to unexplained reasons by the RAF. From Australia, I was temporarily, attached to the Air Ministry Unit at RAF Uxbridge, and they would inform me of my new unit before my leave expired. The day before my leave expiry, I still had not heard a word, so I sent them a telegram requesting the info. I received a reply the next day telling me to stay at home until they could get the details from the Air Ministry London. After almost three weeks, the reply came; I should report to 46 Squadron, Fighter Command, RAF Odiham on August 15th 1957. I should also keep the telegrams as authority to claim the extra ration and travelling allowances. Not a bad deal all round, 20 days extra leave and a posting just 35 miles from home. When I eventually reported to 46 Squadron, they wanted to know where I had been, as they had been expecting me three weeks ago. I am not sure that they believed me until I showed them the telegrams.

This was to be another interesting period, 46 Sqdn was equipped with Gloster Meteor Night Fighters Mk.NF11, and were now in the process of re-equipping with Gloster Javelin Mk.1and Mk.2s.

These were the first RAF delta wing fighters with night fighting capabilities. This would no doubt mean many night shifts!

It had been an interesting year, and looked as if the next one would also be in the same category!

Reg Simpson

Chapter 9: You Will Be Safe!

Many years later and much wiser, if we review that comment made by Wing/Cmdr. Urquhart, *'You will be safe'*. Just how safe were we?

When applied to the 'decontam' crew in particular, there does not appear to be any authoritative answer. The very subject of the probability of genetic defects being passed down to our descendants, due to the probable physiological damage caused by excessive exposure to radiation to our bodies, opens a very large political can of worms. There does not appear to have been any assessment made public by any organisation or British government, as to the effects of prolonged exposure to radioactively contaminated water upon the human body. The duplicity of successive British governments and their civil service advisers is almost unbelievable when it comes to the matter of the potential damage of radiation to health, suffered by veterans of the British nuclear tests. Their continual denial of liability is a source of anger and frustration by veterans, who suspect the British government believe that by continual denial, the few surviving veterans that remain will soon die off and the problem will disappear.

When one compares the British government's infantile attitudes to the mature attitude of many other nuclear governments, who openly admit liability in that damage was, or may have been, caused to their veteran's health through involvement in their nuclear tests. Many veterans wonder about the various ailments they suffer from, and if there is any radiation link. One of my colleagues on the decontam crew succumbed after several years to stomach and colon cancer after the tests. Another, developed lung and stomach cancers and eventually died.

As for myself, I developed prostate cancer in 2004 which for which I underwent prostatectomy. Now, 10 years on, I have recurrent

Reg Simpson

prostate cancer. This is when, as there is no prostate the cancer
spreads to other parts of the body. Was this the result of those
'irradiated showers'? I don't know, maybe, maybe not. In all
probability I will never know for certain!

Currently, I am having treatment to keep the cancer under control.
This treatment is in the form of hormone injections, the hormones
prevent my body from producing testosterone.

There are side effects, i.e. breast enlargement. This does not bother
me, although some might be envious. I keep a close eye on my
choice of clothing; to ensure that I do not slip on a pair of high
heels and a pretty, floral dress with matching handbag; and go
tottering off down to the local shops. My wife's underwear drawer
is strictly 'off limits' to me, so no danger from there.
I have warned my GP, that if I turn up in his surgery wearing the
above outfit or similar, that it will be a sign that I've had too much
hormone treatment. On the other hand, dressing in that manner
might be a good idea. I could then claim 'minority group status',
and would be assured that I would be recognised and treated
sympathetically, as opposed to being a British Nuclear Test
Veteran.

To some people it may appear that I am treating a serious illness
with some frivolity. To others it may appear to be a bit politically
incorrect. Nevertheless, I still have a sense of humour, and it
further brightens my day, to have a dose of military type humour.
Why should this be any different?
Minority groups? Political correctness? Well, what can one say?
We are talking about the real world, not some pussyfooting,
pansyish, make believe world for the abnormal of our species.

The British Nuclear Test Veterans Association formed in 1983, to
provide a contact point for veterans. The Association aims are to

campaign for recognition and compensation for those veterans and their descendants suffering with illnesses related to the veterans service on those nuclear tests.

After leaving the service and the many years that have since elapsed, I look back on those experiences with some fondness. I truly did enjoy my time during 'Operation Buffalo' at Maralinga, it may only have lasted for three months but it was probably the highlight of my eight years in the RAF. It was an exciting time, and in many ways a privilege to have been part of that particular event.

Reg Simpson

References

There is a mass of information on the internet regarding nuclear testing. To find more information about the British Nuclear test programmes and its' veterans, search on the internet for the following:

The following list is but a few sites:

British Nuclear Test Veterans Association (website: bntva.com)

www.nuclearweaponarchive.org

General internet search – 'Maralinga'

Reg Simpson

Glossary

An explanation, of terms and abbreviations used in this book for those not of the RAF persuasion.

Ranks:

AC2...Aircraftman 2nd Class

(Lowest form of RAF life)

AC1...Aircraftman 1st Class

LAC...Leading Aircraftman

SAC ....Senior Aircraftman

J/T ....Junior Technician

CPL..Corporal*

SGT ....Sergeant*

F/SGT...Flight Sergeant*

W/O ....Warrant Officer*

(Highest rank in Non-Commissioned Officers '*')

SWO ....Station Warrant Officer
(Usually reckoned to be the most powerful rank on any unit, sometimes referred to as God)

NCO ....Non-Commissioned Officers*

P/OFF...Pilot Officer

(Lowest form of Officer life)

F/OFF...Flying Officer

(One step up from Pilot Officer)

SQDN/LDR ....Squadron Leader

(mid-Senior Officer)

WING/CMDR .... Wing Commander

(Senior Officer)

W/C ....Abbreviation for Wing Commander

WINGCO ....Slang for W/C

Reg Simpson

Glossary <small>cont'd</small>

G/ CAPT..Group Captain

(Most senior Officer below 'Air' rank)

Miscellaneous:

BODS .... .Bodies

CO .... ….....…......Commanding Officer

FEAF..Far East Air Force

HMT ....…...............Her Majesty's Troopship

MEAF..Middle East Air Force

NAAFI ....…..Navy Army Air Force Institute

(Canteen)

MU ....…....Maintenance Unit

RNAF ....…..…..Royal Nederland Air Force

SNOWDROPS ....RAF Police

(Derogatory term - due of the white tops to their hats.)

SQDN ....…..……Abbreviation for Squadron

Epilogue

Writing this has been a welcome opportunity for me, to be selfish and reminisce with myself, about those exciting times nearly sixty years ago when I was less worldly wise and possibly more foolhardy. On the other hand, I did volunteer to join the RAF in 1951 and serve my country, come what may.

To all my colleagues from those Maralinga days with 76 Sqdn, I apologise should I not have mentioned you by name, but frankly, I can still see your faces, but the names in the main, escape me.
You may have the same lapses of attention to detail as I do. Do not worry, the condition, is more commonly known as convenient memory loss, or maybe, protection of the innocent. Of course, I have not covered fully all those escapades at Maralinga; anonymity is a useful tool sometimes.
Should 'Martin' by any chance read this; I hope his career progressed onto the stages of carrying 'heavy gold braid'.

With the changes in the status of BNTVA to a registered charity, the website no longer has the facility for personal contact. It is regrettable that veterans have not been able to maintain contact with one another via the guestbook. We must all now be in our 80s, so it will be inevitable that some will have not made it this far, for whatever reason. I salute them, whether they went 'upstairs', or down to that other place!

Whichever crew room is to be my final destination, be it 'up', or 'down', please don't hog all the space, shuffle up a bit and make room. I am still a tall skinny – well almost, but grey haired wrinkly

Reg Simpson

old 'git', who can still make the coffee in exchange for a seat on the board!